Swinging Pendulums

SWINGING PENDULUMS

Cautionary Tales for Early Childhood Education

CAROL GARHART MOONEY

Redleaf Press®
www.redleafpress.org
800-423-8309

Published by Redleaf Press
10 Yorkton Court
St. Paul, MN 55117
www.redleafpress.org

First edition 2012
Cover design by Jim Handrigan
Cover photograph © Image Source Photography/Veer
Interior design by Jim Handrigan
Typeset in Minion Pro
Printed in the United States of America
18 17 16 15 14 13 12 11   1 2 3 4 5 6 7 8

"Children's Needs for Development" was first published in *Talks with Teachers: Reflections on Early Childhood Education* by Lilian Katz (Washington, DC: National Association for the Education of Young Children, 1977). Reprinted with permission from the author.

Library of Congress Cataloging-in-Publication Data
Mooney, Carol Garhart.
   Swinging pendulums : cautionary tales for early childhood education / Carol Garhart Mooney.
      p. cm.
   Includes bibliographical references.
   ISBN 978-1-60554-080-1 (alk. paper)
   1. Early childhood education—United States. 2. Educational change—United States.   I. Title.
   LB1139.25.M59 2012
   372.210973—dc23
                                                                2011026346

Printed on acid-free paper

This book is dedicated with admiration and gratitude to Wendy Kessler for her lifetime career investment in regulating and improving the quality of programs for young children and their families.

CONTENTS

Like most early childhood educators, I have been influenced by Lilian Katz and her contributions to our field. For years, I have listened to her mindful cautions to bring balance to our work with young children and their families. I have heard her say that within the solution to each problem are the seeds for better alternatives—and new problems. I have heard her say, "It's only a mistake if you don't learn from it." I agree with Katz when she suggests that too many of us suffer from "analysis paralysis." We allow ourselves to overthink many issues, becoming so afraid of doing the wrong thing that we do nothing instead. Even an error in our judgment teaches children that we have the courage to take action. That is setting a good example even if, in retrospect, a different action would have been a better choice.

A willingness to laugh at ourselves is important. I have been told on more than one occasion that I am an overachiever in this area. It is true that I love to be funny, and this will be apparent to you in the essays that follow. But I humbly and very seriously assure you that my intent with this book is to urge all of us to be mindful, courageous, and responsible in addition to lighthearted when approaching our work. In no way am I trying to poke fun at rules, regulations, guidelines, or outstanding practices. Instead, I am giving a call for intentional teaching. I'm urging us all to have the courage to be imperfect. I'm saying that sometimes doing the wrong thing for the right reason is okay.

Undeniably, our individual culture, age or stage, family, or temperament can lead us to respond to a scenario in a way we generally would not. In the 1970s, for example, I administered district-required tests to second graders. In one section of the test, children were instructed to circle one of four illustrated boats, whichever one appeared different from the others. I could see that color—three of the boats were green and one was red—was meant to be the distinctive element. One of my most capable students, however, circled one of the green boats instead of the glaring red one. My history with the child made me look twice; the boat he circled was larger than the other three! He taught me to be more thoughtful.

It is in this spirit of mindfulness that I offer these stories. I hope they will be thought provoking. The particular essay topics were selected because many teachers talk about them; they were not selected for any other reason. It is not my intent to present them as lessons or problems needing immediate solutions. I just hope they make people think and talk, and I hope they will be used—as my editor Kyra Ostendorf suggests—as "book club" readings for early childhood educators. I want the essays to promote discussions about some of the issues that affect our daily work with children. Because so many of the topics came directly from discussions with providers, I know they are topics that interest, irritate, or intrigue teachers. Some of the essays are long and offer conclusions to some extent. Some are very short and only raise questions. The essays can be read in random order or sequentially. They can be discussed as a group or pondered individually.

Jonathan Kozol once suggested that teacher behaviors are the secret curriculum we share with children every day. I quite agree with him and think both teachers and children can benefit from our attempts to expose our secrets and learn from them.

ACKNOWLEDGMENTS

Many people are involved in the creation of a book. David Heath and Kyra Ostendorf at Redleaf Press have been there with humor, support, and guidance since the beginning. I thank Denise Corvino for her encouragement when discussing ideas considered too controversial by some. I thank Wendy Kessler, Katie Miller, and Kathy O'Neill for years of advice and guidance on regulating programs that serve young children and their families. I am grateful to the New Hampshire Child Care Resource and Referral Network for bringing providers together in focus groups to discuss what troubles them; I am grateful to Cindy Wallace for arranging those groups.

People both at work and at home offer the extra help, understanding, and friendship that keep me going—in "book years" and in life. You know who you are.

Carol Garhart Mooney
Barnstead, New Hampshire
2011

An Obituary for Common Sense

T he seminar was on emergency evacuation plans and procedures for child care programs. It was late in the afternoon after a long day at the center. I was surprised by the number of other directors choosing to finish their long day at this workshop, but since September 11, 2001, it seemed we were all feeling the responsibility to be adequately prepared for emergencies. I didn't have high expectations for the presentation because the subject seemed quite dry, so I was delighted to find the safety official articulate, interesting, and humorous. Emergency evacuation is not a particularly funny topic, which makes what happened at this training quite remarkable. The speaker got over a hundred professionals to laugh at their own follies, and that gave me the inspiration to write this book.

The speaker had a wealth of experience with natural disasters, including floods, hurricanes, and fires, and with a range of other problems, including gas leaks, airplane crashes, and bomb threats. He urged us to remain calm in front of children, to think on our feet, and to use common sense during emergencies. It was the common sense part—and his examples of situations where it was lacking—that brought down the house, causing us to wipe tears of laughter from our eyes. It was the kind of boisterous laughter that is laced with the recognition of one's own foolishness. This group had seen and participated in everything he was describing. Fortunately, most of our foolish personal experiences did not occur in crisis situations.

The speaker seriously discussed the responsibility we all share to help children feel safe and be safe as best we can, but his observations of early childhood educators in crisis situations gave him much fear. He described a particularly poignant scene: "Try to picture the child care center at the World Trade Center on September 11," he said to us. "Imagine the firefighter's angst when a teacher said to him, 'I'd love to help you with the children's evacuation, but you need to remember that state regulations require a car seat for every toddler and a booster seat for all four- and five-year-olds'!"

Again and again, the speaker recounted tales of fires, floods, and tornados during which educators were firm that children could not be released until adult–child ratios aligned with state licensing regulations. In emergency situations, educators were firm that the number of car seats and booster seats needed to match the ages and weights of the children before they could take action. He made fun of us in a playful but thought-provoking way. As I drove home that night, I reflected on the presentation. Even though I enjoyed both its serious and humorous aspects, I thought about the broader implications of an early childhood practice without common sense. I wasn't chuckling.

A few weeks later, I read Lori Borgman's essay titled "The Death of Common Sense" in the *Indianapolis Star* (March 15, 1998). The author writes an obituary for Common Sense as if it were a person who died. It's a funny and poignant essay, and it had such relevant connections to the workshop I attended. It also reminded me that the potential for harm increases when we forgo common sense.

When it comes to common sense, early childhood educators need a double dose. Why? We have spent decades trying to get professional communities to take us seriously. We do serious, important work that the general public often trivializes. Perhaps this is why we have struggled more than any other group to know what to call ourselves. In my lifetime, we have run the gamut from calling everyone in the building "teacher" to establishing hierarchies ranging from "aides" to "lead teachers." We often wonder which function of our positions we should focus on when establishing our job titles. If we work in child care, do we call ourselves "caregivers" or "educators" or both? Magda Gerber introduced the title "educarer." Years ago, the general public routinely called early childhood educators "day care workers."

I know colleagues who come close to cardiac arrest at the sound of the word *day care*. I'm all for raising professional standards, but I also question the logic of correcting local businesspeople who are working with us on funding or legislation when they use the word *day care*. Institutional memory dies hard, and for years *day care* was not considered a bad word. Our esteemed colleague Gwen Morgan published a groundbreaking and helpful manual called *Managing the Day Care Dollars*. No one questions the integrity of Fred Rogers, a true champion for children, who wrote a children's book called *Going to Day Care*. It was simply a different time. I use *child care* because I like it, but I don't consider it an insult when someone uses *day care*, and I never correct people in a public place for using that historic term.

I am not suggesting, of course, that we return to old policies or terminology that have been improved upon over the years. Seasoned early childhood educators tremble, for example, at how we used to transport children in cars. In the 1960s, we'd fill the back of a station wagon with a dozen children and be on our way to the zoo! We didn't think of ourselves as irresponsible. Cars didn't come with seat belts. Infant seats were not yet an option. We are glad for the improvements that have been made, and today we insist that children buckle up. We also acknowledge that our primitive practices were the best we had at the time.

Most seasoned educators also admit to each other that for some early childhood principles the swinging pendulum of opinion has swung too far to extremes, in one direction or the other. We look at each other, baffled, when a behavioral expert at a conference suggests that we should never say "no" to young children. These pundits say, "Find a way to phrase it in the positive!" As a general rule, I agree with this statement, but when it comes to woodstoves, traffic, or poking a friend in the eye with a stick—well, you get the point.

A respected colleague of many years cautioned me, "I hope you don't get yourself in trouble with this new book. People can get so agitated about things, and it sounds like you're opening some cans of worms." It is my intent to open minds. I'd like providers to debate some of the controversial subjects presented. The essays are sometimes tongue in cheek, but they are always meant to be thought-provoking looks at how to make sensible decisions for the children and families in our care. The issues discussed in this book are the ones that stood out to me as I contemplated policies that foster extremism. The essays welcome discussion, not study. They are not intended as guidelines or directives. They are observations that have triggered reactions and conversations. It is my hope that you will stop to think about some of these common "swinging pendulum" issues that affect our work with children on a daily basis. I think we need to take ourselves seriously as professionals, but taking ourselves too seriously can be, well, extreme. Read through the essays. Talk with your colleagues. Laugh a little. See if you can find a few places where you can add a dash of common sense. Enjoy!

❡

PROFESSIONALISM

❡

1

Teachers and Learners

In 1968, I was in charge of my first class. I had thirty-eight third graders in my care. Some children came from wealthy families, others lived in poverty. In those days, we didn't label children as having attention deficit disorder (ADD), oppositional defiant disorder (ODD), or attention deficit/hyperactive disorder (ADHD). Not many connections had been made between low birth weight, prenatal care, lead poisoning, or socioeconomic status and children's learning. We didn't speak of outcomes, responsive classrooms, or individualized education programs. We did have a parent-teacher organization (PTO) that cleaned up the playground. That playground was on asphalt—not on eight inches of "child-friendly" bark mulch.

I had never heard of Howard Gardner, but I tried to convince Timmy's dad that Timmy was gifted in artistic expression, even though he struggled in math. I tried to help Laura's parents see that she could hit a baseball and slam-dunk a basketball, even though spelling was difficult for her. I saw parents as the key to children's success. I tried to look at what children *could* do instead of what they couldn't. Parents didn't always see it that way. They got frustrated. I got discouraged, and I panicked.

"I don't know what to do!" I exclaimed to my grandmother over the phone. My grandmother had taught in a one-room schoolhouse at the turn of the last century. I explained, "Some children can do so much, and some can do so little. Some are really rude to me, and I don't know what to do. I get scared." Grandma was brisk and not too sympathetic. She told me, "Your class is no different than mine was.

The age children really are (chronological) and the age they function at (developmental) can really be quite different. The best way to be an effective teacher is to really get to know them (observe and assess; watch carefully and write down what you see). You need an accurate picture of their abilities right now. Then you can develop a plan for taking them further. Remember, they will get taller and older without your guidance, but not kinder or smarter—that's your job!"

Now I am a grandmother, and my grandchildren say that I must be a good teacher because I am funny! I am also the school administrator of a small early childhood program. A few of our families live in poverty. Some families have middle-range incomes. All of them are worried about their children. Some children are right on target developmentally, and some are seriously behind their peers. All of them are more interested in the paving crew working on our driveway than the developmentally appropriate curriculum the teachers have prepared. Some children have had breakfast; others have not. Some live in struggling neighborhoods where their evening lullabies are the sounds of police car sirens and breaking whiskey bottles. Our more fortunate parents have stable employment but are already worried about SAT scores, anorexia, and peer pressure. The parents want to buy dolls, books, and balls for the children. The children want iPads, Kindles, and cell phones. Everything seems to move at a pace none of us can keep up with.

Wanting to do well by children and their families, teachers come to me and ask, "What should I do?" I tell them that being an educator is a big job. SAUs (school administrative units) have expectations. Parents have expectations. Families differ in what they want for their children. Children have differing abilities. But all children have stories to tell; try to listen. All children have fears; try to ease them. All children have abilities; try to nurture them. I tell teachers that sometimes the responsibility can be scary. We don't always know or understand the best route to take, and we all have different talents. We need to heed the words of the brilliant Maya Angelou (Tate 1983, 6): "Talent is like electricity. We don't understand electricity. We use it." I tell the teachers not to spend too much time trying to understand every piece of the puzzle. I tell them to focus, instead, on using their talents and on teaching the children to recognize and use their own. We can overthink almost anything—and suffer from analysis paralysis as Lilian Katz suggests—and scare ourselves into doing nothing. I believe my grandmother was right: watch children carefully, take note of their strengths, and then take them a little further.

Teacher preparation is a huge responsibility. Future educators need to be inspired and challenged. They must learn how to implement an intentional, mindful methodology while preparing for the day-to-day reality of classroom life. To ignore the impact of budgets, standards, federal and state regulations, bureaucrats, and other contemporary barriers to effective teaching is to deny the totality of our work. Balancing professional enthusiasm and trust with caution and reality is essential. I am discouraged at how often I see the bright lights of brand-new teachers burning out within months of real classroom work. The research is pretty clear that few trained teachers end up having the stamina to stay in teaching (Wong and Wong 2009). One reason for this, I believe, is that we are not honest enough about the reality of the job. Now and then, I hear a friend or colleague mention a strategy we used thirty years ago that I know just won't work with today's texting, Skype-ing, and distracted learners. It's hard to keep current when trends change so rapidly, but nowhere is it more necessary than in the profession of shaping the next generation. This is not to say that everything old is no longer relevant, and this is not to say that every new approach is a good one. It does mean we need to be thoughtful and reflective.

Years ago at a National Association for the Education of Young Children (NAEYC) conference, I heard someone say that teacher educators should have to teach for an entire semester every five years to maintain their credentials. I agreed with the statement then, and I believe it to be more necessary now. When teacher educators observe their students in classrooms for two hours, two or three times a semester, in an unfamiliar setting, it's impossible for them to feel the current trends of children as learners and of schools as places of learning.

One thing that has not changed in early childhood education—though I wish it would—is the desire for easy answers. Twenty years ago, student teachers would ask me, "What works?" and then hope

9

I'd give an answer. Today they still ask me, "What works?" They don't want to have to think. They ask me questions like these:

- Does it matter if children go down the slide feet first?

- Is time-out a good response to behavioral problems?

- Should I make children listen to a story even if they aren't interested?

- Should I try to teach reading to a child who doesn't have a solid prereading foundation?

My answer, "It depends," is always a disappointment, but it's honest. There are many things it depends on.

Here are a few of the elements necessary for providing quality educational experiences to all children:

- Teachers need to know about children's growth and development.

- Teachers need to be well educated in the areas where they are expected to perform.

- Teachers need to be energized and well rested, and they must want to work with children.

- Teachers need to be mentored, coached, supported, and given time to reflect together on their work with children.

- Teachers need adequate benefits and compensation.

- Teachers need to be held accountable.

- Teachers need ongoing, meaningful professional development opportunities, no matter how many years they have been teaching.

- Children need to be safe, well rested, and adequately fed to focus on learning.

- Children need teachers who understand their developmental stage as well as their chronological age.

- Children need to feel confident that their family is respected.

Here are some of the barriers to positive educational experiences for all:

- poverty

- violence

- indifference

- inadequate resources

- mediocre teachers

- inappropriate curricula

- poorly maintained buildings

- inadequate enthusiasm

- low expectations for achievement

Even by just tackling the items in these limited lists, we could change the competence of the next generation and reduce dropout and incarceration rates. As several committed charter schools and public schools have proven, with high expectations and significant financial and human resources, all children in the United States could receive what they deserve—quality education—and develop the abilities they are born with.

The impact of changing times and family styles, as well as cultural and educational influences on teaching, has created a world for educators that is different from the one my grandmother inhabited. We can still impact that different world. My grandmother's long-ago words still ring with the truth of teaching well: "Children will get taller and older without your help, but not kinder or smarter—that's your job!"

Questions for Discussion

1. Do you think teacher wages make a difference in the quality of education that children receive?

2. If poverty is a variable affecting education, what can teachers do to eliminate it?

3. Is experience in working with young children as valuable as academic preparation in early childhood growth, development, and education? Why or why not?

It's Not a Career
for the Weak of Heart

I really didn't want to go. I had been an early childhood educator for more than thirty years. I read the books. I went to all the conferences. I knew the issues. What could Louise Stoney, cofounder of the Alliance for Early Childhood Finance, tell me that I didn't already know? Besides, for the past three days, it had been too cold for the children to go outside; a well-loved teacher announced her retirement; and I had to call the facilities manager three times to unplug toilets that had received a drop of Duplo blocks. So, I really didn't want to go.

But I'm an early childhood educator. I love my work. I'm committed to children and those who care for and educate them. I feel a professional responsibility to my colleagues. For younger professionals, I feel a responsibility to model the untiring persistence required to work in our industry. My professional association, Early Learning NH, was sponsoring the event. So I went.

With a simplicity unusual in our field and with a clarity that professional journals, graduate courses, and other seminars had failed to achieve, Louise Stoney described the challenge of quality care and education for young children: "Regardless of age, gender, ethnicity, or socioeconomic status, if you ask a person on the street the difference between a Hyundai and a BMW, they can tell you. But if you ask a person on the street the difference between poor quality and high quality in child care, they don't know what to say!" In my experience, I have found that many consumers and providers of child care services are also unsure of the difference.

I was glad I went. I took notes furiously. I drove home thinking, "I need to do something with this." When I got home, I set the notes on my desk alongside the piles of research due to my publisher by August, the unfinished syllabus due to my college by June, the presentation due to the funders of my program by next Saturday, and the birthday card due to my son last weekend! Weeks passed. March came in like a lion after a relatively tame winter. I had an open house at work to boost enrollment. I worked on my book, my syllabus, and the bad cold I caught from the children who keep me coming back to the job I love. I planned a big-sister shower for a child in our program who would soon be one. My notes from Louise Stoney's presentation sat under a pile of more pressing paperwork. I went searching for my notes in the spring when a media blitz on the research of Jay Belsky et al. (2007) hit the Internet, ABC, CBS, NBC, and FOX, as well as the *New York Times*.

The public approach to sharing information on child care has always seemed inflammatory, negative, and unsupportive of working families and child care professionals. I once saw an article with the headline "Working Mom versus Stay at Home Mom." The article was accompanied by a photograph of women in boxing gloves fighting in a ring. Another article featured a photo of a mom snuggling her little ones while reading to them; steaming cocoa sits on the coffee table as they all enjoy a roaring fire from the fireplace. The headline read, "Remember When Moms Kept the Home Fires Burning: Who Cares for America's Children?"

Where are the photos of the dads who alter career plans to care for their young? Where are the grandparent photos? Where are the stories about the passion, commitment, and planning that well-educated men and women put into creating quality care for children? The whole story is never told, and the lack of balanced information about child care impacts families and providers in the United States:

- It creates fear and guilt.

- It scares loving grandparents into pressuring their adult children to quit jobs they need—or love—to stay at home.

- It reflects poorly on adults who have chosen child care as their life's work.

- It reinforces the idea that there is "natural and expected tension" between parents and providers.

Reflecting on all of this leads me back to that seminar with Louise Stoney, to the Hyundai and BMW, and to the differences between quality care, mediocre care, and poor care for young children.

I'm going to go out on a limb here. I have no formal research of my own to base this on, but I have raised four children, I am a grand-mother, and I have the qualitative research of four decades of actually working with children and their families. I have worked in urban and rural areas; low- and high-income neighborhoods; accredited and nonaccredited settings; and family care, group care, Head Start, and university laboratory schools. In the 1970s, I read Selma Fraiberg's in-depth studies confirming that the majority of care in the United States was not high quality. I have kept up with the new studies that tell us not enough has changed. But I also know this to be true: there is quality care, mediocre care, and poor care in child care *and* in homes.

What we focus on we give power to and get more of. When we approach the challenge of offering the next generation the best possible outcomes by asking, "Should this take place at home or should this take place in group care?" we are focusing on the wrong question. Our focus truly needs to be on answering these: What promotes the best possible outcomes for children? How do we, the people (teachers, nurses, moms, dads, grandparents, child care providers, police officers, older siblings, neighbors, aunties, coaches, advertisers, pediatricians, and so on), create more environments that promote the best outcomes for children (both our own children and other people's)? What are the critical and ever-changing needs of the next generation? How do all of us work together to make high-quality education more abundant and equitably delivered? These are the essential challenges for those who care for and care about the next generation.

Questions for Discussion

1. Has your center ever written out a description of quality child care services? If not, how easy would it be for you to write the description together?

2. Why does the general public know what quality means for automobiles, construction, home repair, and medical services but not for child care?

3. Why does our media jump on every instance of aggressive behavior, sexual assault, and contagious illness in child care settings but choose to ignore these problems in homes, where they exist in equal numbers?

3

Help Wanted: Early Childhood Educator for Limited Hours in a Small, Quality Setting

For as long as I can remember, people have been saying, "You can't get good help these days." But a recent attempt to hire a part-time closer at my center has given me pause to reflect on how much more complicated this problem is in early childhood education (ECE) than in some other fields.

I have long been fond of Ellen Galinsky's (1999) term for the last hour of the day in child care; she calls it the "arsenic hour." Those of us who work in child care know how hard this time of the day is. The children are tired. The teachers are tired. There might be tension between openers and closers if housekeeping chores haven't been done quite right. At the sight of their parents, children who have been great all day melt down, often running, hiding, or acting out. Parents are exhausted and tense after battling rush-hour traffic to get to the center by closing time. They might feel sad and embarrassed when their little ones don't act happy to see them, especially if the staff is not well trained in end-of-the-day support strategies for children and parents.

So, let's see, the best possible candidate for this end-of-the-day position is a veteran early childhood educator. This person has parent-support training and, even though we are not supposed to say it, children of his or her own who sometimes act out at inopportune moments. The candidate also has the patience of Job, the humor of Ellen DeGeneres, and the energy and physical flexibility of Jim Carrey or Robin Williams. Experience at Merry Maids would also help at cleanup time.

My advertisement specified that an associate's degree was required—though a bachelor's degree was preferred—in ECE or a related field, with salary commensurate to both education and experience. It occurred to me when I started fielding inquiries from people who worked at national chain restaurants and people who had master's degrees in ethics of modern medicine that I didn't repeat "experience in early childhood education" frequently enough in the ad. As a clue, I often use only the abbreviation ECE in ads and during interviews. If you don't know what ECE stands for, well, your application goes into the circular file with the one from the young woman claiming to be a "sofmor" at a local college.

The most discouraging and perplexing questions, however, came from those with associate's degrees or more in ECE or related fields. One young woman asked, "When you say limited hours, I assume you mean morning preschool?" I responded, "Well, no, it's actually a closing position." The young woman seemed more impatient than disappointed. In an unpleasant tone, she asserted, "Well, then, why did you describe the position as one for an educator? I want to teach! I have a bachelor's degree in ECE. I'm not a babysitter."

I have always been a fan of teachable moments because they remind me that there is no right time of day for teaching young children. I remember well-planned learning times with my own kids, such as visits to historic sites, museums, and science centers, that went awry. I also remember the many philosophical discussions and life lessons that took place in the car—stopped in traffic—on the way to cross-country meets, music lessons, or the grocery store. Children are always watching us and learning from us. A favorite expression of mine is bumper-sticker wisdom, "Children learn from example. The problem is they don't know a good one from a bad one!"

Returning to the part-time position and the impatient candidate, I defend my response to her by saying it occurred during the arsenic hour. It was the end of a long day, and I really needed to fill the position soon. The whiner on the other end of the phone went on to describe her fine resume, her vast experience in teaching young children, and how misleading the advertisement was. I said, in an impatient tone of my own, "So, these skills of yours can only be used before noon?" There was a moment of silence, an insincere "Thank you," and a *click*.

This woman was not the only candidate who considered the word *educator* misleading because the position was for a late-afternoon shift. She also was not the only candidate to assert that she wasn't looking for a babysitting job and that she wanted to teach. I guess I would have understood the confusion if it had come from the restaurant guy who thought it would be fun to work with kids (How hard could it be, anyway?). What troubled me was that trained ECE people were confused. What college program in ECE ever suggested that children only learn in the morning? The confusion raised so many questions in my mind:

- What about the importance of fostering family connections at the end of the day?

- What about the child whose family is late for pickup? Does it not take skill to handle that situation well?

- What about the skills needed to get the reluctant child out of the center tactfully?

- What about the ability to "let go" and leave the center less tidy than you'd like to—with a quick note to your opening colleague—because the afternoon was tough and there were late pickups?

- What about the fact that drop-off and pickup times are the primary windows through which parents view the world their children inhabit day after day?

Don't these things make a closing professional as essential to program quality as an opener? If so, why do so many programs fill this crucial time with inexperienced staff?

Fortunately, the position was filled by someone with outstanding credentials and experience. She didn't want many hours. She didn't need the job; she wanted it! She was thrilled to be a part of our team. This educator's experience was at very high-quality programs. During the interview, she reflected sadly, "Working at those programs kind of ruined me. I tried several jobs, but so many sites just didn't take the work seriously." In the interim, she had taken time off. I was curious, so I asked, "What made you respond to our ad?" She said, "It was simple, really. You acknowledged the importance of both education and experience, and you used the words *educator* and *limited hours*. That told me you knew what we wish everyone who works with children would remember: Children are always watching and always learning. Every minute counts!"

"You're hired," I said.

Questions for Discussion

1. Have you ever worked in a setting that has salary differentials between child care teachers and prekindergarten/kindergarten teachers? Why do you think this policy was in place? Was it justified?

2. How does knowledge of early childhood education differ from experience in working with young children? Is one of these more desirable than the other?

3. Do people in our field think experience is more important than education or vice versa? Why?

4

Worthy Wages: How Long Can We Afford to Ignore Them?

I was listening to a National Public Radio (NPR) affiliate's special on child care, in which budgets, national and local, were repeatedly mentioned. An early childhood colleague, Jackie Cowell (2011), talked about the worthy wage campaign, which spurred an immediate flash of history for me. She spoke to the old verse we all knew in the 1980s: "Parents can't afford to pay. Teachers can't afford to stay. There's got to be a better way!" I shook my head and thought, "Same old, same old." Then I was sad.

I have spent forty years working in schools, child care centers, the state government, and colleges. The education and care of children and families has been my family business. I am the third generation of my family in education, and my children are the fourth. Last week, my youngest daughter, who will receive a master's degree in education in June from a fine university, spoke with me about her career direction. Since earning her bachelor's degree three years ago, she has taught in the inner city of Chicago. She now plans to return to the East Coast to continue her work in education and urban poverty. As a parent, I worry about her personal poverty!

When teaching first-year college students, I am always alarmed by the pride with which they say, "I am not in it for the money!" Some students drop my course after that first class when I try to convince them that this is not such a healthy mantra. I ask them, "You don't worry about driving a car that runs well and is reliable in bad weather?" A frequent response is, "No, I'm saying I don't need a BMW." I remind

21

students that in New Hampshire we have dangerous driving conditions from November until March; this is not a place for worn tires! Plus, gas isn't cheap. I then ask my students how many of them still live with their parents. Due to their stage in life, most of them respond in the affirmative. Next, I ask if they know the cost of a two-bedroom house in their community and rent for a studio apartment. Year after year, my students' guesses are nowhere near the actual costs. Having been a mother of young adults for the past fifteen years, I stay in touch with this pricing!

I then move on to health care and its importance. Many young people tell me that health care costs are an obsession of older people like me. They tell me, "Our generation is healthier. Besides, we can stay on our parents' policies until we turn twenty-six." At eighteen, most of these new college students have no idea how quickly twenty-six will come. My youngest daughter turns twenty-five this year, so we will be able to carry her on our insurance for only one more year. Her benefits package is of great interest to me as she prepares to make serious career choices. It concerns me that she is more concerned with saving the world than being able to insure her own health. When our discussions get heated, she says, "Maybe you shouldn't have sent me to schools that focus on giving back. I thought you wanted me to care."

In these moments, I become speechless and feel sad, much like I did this morning when the radio program suggested there weren't any wage improvements in sight. It is probably trite to mention the contrast between the salaries of child care workers and those of athletes, music idols, and people in the upper 2 percent of incomes in the United States. It is true that I wanted my daughter to grow up to care, but being able to care and being able to take care of oneself should not be incompatible goals.

We are missing something in teacher education if we skip over the importance of advocating for better wages. It is true that we can make do on less, but it is also true that we are all going to have to get better at doing just that. Choosing to educate and care for the next generation should not mean surrendering the ability to support oneself, and it should not mean giving up dreams of a modest home, a garden, and a car that runs. The challenge to advocate for better wages for early childhood professionals should be every American's responsibility.

When my daughter was trying to choose a major, she pondered early childhood education. I said I didn't mind an early childhood concentration, but I told her she needed to get certified in elementary or middle school education as well. It was hard for me to say out loud that I wasn't paying her college tuition so she could work in a profession where 50 percent of employers don't offer benefits, paid vacation, or reasonable wages. I felt like a traitor to my own field, but I'm a parent, and I needed to say it. So she got the degree in elementary education, went to the inner city, and enjoyed free group housing for two years as part of a service project. The first year she paid rent, I received random phone messages from her. Instead of "Hello," I would hear a distressed voice saying something like, "Do you know how much two chicken breasts cost? Call me!" Now new challenges are on the horizon for my daughter as she discusses doctorate programs in urban poverty. The mother inside me raises awful questions like, "What does one do with a doctorate in urban poverty, and what does it pay?"

Last month, my middle son paid for my daughter to fly to the East Coast to hear Geoffrey Canada deliver an inspiring lecture at his place of employment. She called me afterward, and with intelligence, exuberance, and caring she exclaimed, "There is a man who knows what we need to do for children! I wish you could have had the day off to hear him, Mom. It was so inspirational." I have heard Geoffrey Canada speak at NAEYC conventions, and my daughter is right—he is both accurate in his assessment of education in the United States and inspiring. But I was unable to go to Boston for that particular speech because my husband and I were busy participating in our own version of the government's "cash for clunkers" program. My youngest son's truck died, so we were out paying cash for a new car in order to give him our clunker! I hear rumors that we will soon be participating in a housing project as well. The tenant will be a good one; she has degrees and good taste, we like her a fair amount, and purple is still her favorite color, so we won't have to repaint!

23

Questions for Discussion

1. Are you and the teachers in your program familiar with the worthy wage campaign and its intent? What do you think of it?

2. Do you think early childhood educators ever act as if making good money is not associated with doing a good job?

3. If a teacher has to work a night shift at the mall to make car payments, do you think it could detract from the quality of his or her work with children during the day? Why?

5

What's in a Name?

Most of us have had children call us "Teacher." It is a big leap for little children to move from the world of "Mommy" or "Grampy" to a busy building full of many adults. Choosing to say "Teacher" might be easier than having to choose between "Mr.," "Ms.," "Miss," or "Mrs." and a variety of first or last names, which may be hard for a young child to pronounce.

In the 1970s, I struggled with families in my preschool who were uncomfortable that I had children call me "Carol." They said, "It seems so disrespectful." I told the families that in my former job as an elementary teacher, I had received many a disrespectful "Mrs. Mooney." In other words, respect is an attitude. It is not a quality inherent in first or last names but a quality in approach. I also shared with them the then popular notion that it was difficult for young children to get used to surnames. First names were supposed to establish intimacy and remove distance between children and their teachers. It didn't occur to me at the time that the children whose parents preferred surnames could have called me "Mrs. Mooney," and the children whose parents preferred informal address could have called me "Carol." My own children were in my preschool group, and they never stopped calling me "Mommy."

Most of us have also had the experience of children calling us "Mommy," giggling at their error, saying "Oops," and then calling us whatever they usually call us. This is normal, and nothing a teacher or parent should worry about. Children are used to calling for their moms, so when they need help in the classroom, it's easy for "Mommy" to be the first word that comes to mind and voice.

Recently, when I heard a respected colleague say, "I would never want a child to call me 'Mrs.' because it sounds so formal," I thought about how I've changed over the decades. At the program where I work, all of the children call teachers "Mr.," "Mrs.," or "Miss" by their last name—it's just how it has always been. There were many things to change when I came on board at this program. I decided this issue didn't have to be one of them. There is much to be said for traditions that don't actually make a huge programmatic difference. Over many years, I have learned to live with things that make me uncomfortable but allow others on staff to be comfortable.

When I attend gatherings at my son's home with his neighbors, I'm always fascinated to hear the children calling adults "Mr. Bob" or "Miss Judy." It's especially the "Miss" that gets to me. These are mostly women one would call "Mrs.," but some of the women are divorced, so do we then go to "Ms."? Maybe I am so used to using first names that I've developed a bias I can't get over. Respect versus disrespect and formality versus informality aside, maybe first names truly are just plain easier. Yet every day children in my program call us "Miss" or "Mrs.," and I've adjusted.

We all know how important names are to very young children. Many young children will follow a total stranger who calls them by name, so this is probably a subject we should give serious consideration. Perhaps individualizing is as important here as it is in skill building. We've all had a Thomas or an Elizabeth who has had a fit if called "Tommy" or "Betty." Asking both children and adults what they prefer to be called is probably the surest and most respectful route of all, but a staff member might speak to "consistency" and upset the balance. This point was driven home to me before my first grandchild was born. My daughter-in-law asked if I had a preference for my grandparent name. Much to my delight, her mother had chosen "Gram," leaving my preference for "Nana" wide open. It wasn't so easy for my husband. His response was "Dave." My daughter-in-law chuckled and said, "No, really, Dave." He replied, "Really. That's my name. Have her call me Dave." The issue of respect came up again. "How about Grandpa Dave?" she asked.

I discussed this dilemma with a colleague, then in her eighties. She was already a great-grandmother. She asked, "What difference does it make? What's in a name? If he wants Dave, let it be Dave! There's a reason for it—there's always a reason. Just ask him." That hadn't occurred to me. As our discussion continued, my friend asked me what Dave had called his grandfather. My puzzled expression turned to a spreading smile. "Jack," I said, "He called him Jack."

This is another example of how we let ourselves get stuck in a belief, practice, rule, or debate—What is the most appropriate way for children to address adults?—without asking the right question. What would you like us to call you? is so simple.

I work in a city where more than fifty languages are spoken in the public schools. It has always been challenging for me to pronounce children's names correctly when I am completely unfamiliar with their home language. It makes me uncomfortable because I respect how important our names are to each of us, so I really try. Some are harder than others, such as with Shirshirchandra. It took the staff a very long time to really get his name right. A year after he had been in our program, his dad came into school beaming. He said, "We want to make a change. We are in America now. We don't want you to use Shirshirchandra. From now on he will have a good American name. Call him Felipe." It was tough, but we made the transition. His family had their story. It was important to them. And when it came time for the children to learn how to write their names, I think Felipe was grateful!

Questions for Discussion

1. Why is what teachers are called so controversial in early childhood programs?

2. Do you prefer formal or informal naming? Why? Is there a consensus on this topic among staff members in your program?

3. If your program's policy is universal—either formal or informal terms of address that everyone must use—how do you explain it to families who disagree with it?

HEALTH AND SAFETY

6

Safety and Regulations

A t a state hearing for child care providers, the chief of the child care licensing bureau fielded questions. "How many minutes do you have to search for a missing child before you are out of compliance?" was one of the first questions. The chief replied, "Well, it depends. How big is your center? Do doors go directly out to fenced-in play areas? Does your environment have comfortable nooks and crannies that a child might head to for solitude? What are your adult–child ratios?" As the chief spoke to the many variables that might affect the situation, her audience became impatient. They wanted a direct and immediate answer with no variables, period. The audience's response reminded me of the student teachers who sometimes say to me, "Just tell me what you want me to do!" I'd respond with the answer they didn't want but came to expect, "Well, it depends!"

Guidelines for keeping children safe, teaching them, and responding to their behavior are much like children's clothing: there's no such thing as one size fits all. Still, there are many important safety questions that can be answered without hesitation:

- Do we let children go into water over their heads if they can't swim? No!

- Do we let a child with a peanut allergy have a tiny bit of peanut butter? No!

- Do we let young children play with fire? No!

- Do we ever hit them? No!

- Do we ever shout at them? . . .

Uh, oh. For the last question, I'm not sure of the answer. We've all had courses giving us recommendations:

- Get down to the child's level.

- Don't shout across the play yard or classroom. Go to the children to speak to them.

- Speak in a conversational tone.

- Don't shout.

These are all good suggestions! But, come on now, let's say you are on the playground and a child throws up. This incident requires the total attention of one teacher. Meanwhile, a parent leaves the gate ajar on the way out, requiring the total attention of another. Then, out of the corner of your eye, you see the youngest three-year-old about to walk in front of a vigorously swinging five-year-old on the swing set. Like most teachers—knowing they couldn't get there in time to scoop the child to safety—you would probably shout. Most of us would agree that you handled the situation in the best possible way. For the last question—Do we ever shout at children?—I think the answer might be, "Possibly, but it's not the best."

Gwen Morgan of Wheelock College in Boston has told many early childhood educators that one of the most helpful skills they can develop is a greater tolerance for ambivalence. *Merriam-Webster's Dictionary* (11th ed.) defines *ambivalence* as "simultaneous and contradictory attitudes or feelings." It's hard to be ambivalent when working with children because fairness and consistency are so important. We want to know the right thing to do, but I agree with Gwen Morgan. There isn't always an easy yes or no answer to the important questions of caring for young children. Sometimes it just depends.

Could this make us look like indecisive educators? I don't know. I'm not sure. Maybe. I think it just depends. I need to get more comfortable with all this!

Questions for Discussion

1. What specific things make you uncomfortable when you are not sure if you are making the "right" choice?

2. What does the old adage "You can't please all of the people all of the time" have to do with our discomfort about making choices?

3. Do you think you or any of your colleagues are looking for easy answers to hard questions? Why?

7

But, Baby, It's Cold Outside!

Child care regulations differ, of course, from state to state. In New England, the handbooks that inform parents of state requirements probably have more references to snow pants than those in Florida, which might emphasize insect repellant and sunblock to equal measure. In the Northeast, to reduce the risk of frostbite, many states regulate the temperature at which children must stay indoors. For years, until enlightened leadership in my state told child care programs to use discretion and common sense, the cutoff was twenty degrees. If it was colder than twenty degrees outside, we had to stay inside.

Those of you who understand microclimates know that there are many factors involved beyond temperature when deciding whether outdoor play is appropriate. A dry ninety-three degrees can be excellent outdoor play weather. A static, humid eighty-seven degrees can be oppressive and a good day for books inside with the air-conditioning (if you're lucky enough to have it!). A bright, sunny, and dry fifteen-degree day can be perfect for sledding or building snowmen, but a damp and chilly twenty-three-degree day with no sun can be miserable.

Individual responses to heat and cold vary greatly as well. I have seen three or four teachers gathered by a window arguing about the exact position of the thermometer. "It looks like twenty-two to me," says the teacher who wears sandals in February. "Don't be silly," says fleece-booted Amanda. "It's nineteen degrees; the sun is shining on the thermometer!"

Children, like teachers, have their preferences. Some children love the cold. Some children love the heat. If we all go outside together for an arbitrarily scheduled playtime, it will be too short for some children and way too long for others. Is it appropriate for children who are freezing and crying to be told repeatedly, "Soon. We are going in soon"? That is, should we rearrange schedules to accommodate children who love outdoor play and don't get cold? Or should we accommodate the children who quickly become uncomfortable in cold temperatures?

Outdoor time is a precious thing that we need to preserve for children, and it is required by most states. Children in full-day care will not get outdoor time unless we make it happen for them. What is a program to do? If you are as fortunate as I am and don't have mandated temperature restrictions, you can do whatever makes sense for the day, the teachers, and your schedule. If you have a mandate, why not try matching staff preferences to the time of year? If you live in San Diego, I guess you can just take equal shifts!

Another option—something I've noticed many programs don't think of—is letting children and teachers who love the outdoors spend more time there, and letting those who prefer the indoors to get a bit of fresh air and then go back inside. Someone on staff is bound to say, "What about schedule? What about consistency?" The challenge for all of us is to break out of mandate mode and make thoughtful decisions that make sense!

Questions for Discussion

1. Do you think outdoor play should be mandated by child care licensing? Why or why not?

2. Does your program schedule specific times for all children to have outside experiences? Is this working? Why or why not?

3. Is time outdoors considered a serious part of your curriculum? How do you know? How is it explained to parents?

8

Nutritious Snacks

Childhood obesity concerns us all. There is no question that most people in the United States eat too much and move too little. Most states offer guidelines to child care programs to help them serve nutritious meals and snacks to children, but sometimes a well-balanced menu and a well-balanced budget don't mix. In programs where meals come from home, many educators offer parents suggestions regarding healthy food choices, but most teachers report that children still frequently bring lunch boxes full of chips, cookies, and assorted nonnutritious, empty-calorie snacks. Should this be a concern to early childhood educators? Even further, how do we respect a family's or culture's food preferences and still be proactive about childhood obesity?

People in the United States seem to have developed an eating disorder the second half of the twentieth century. Before learning their ABCs or how to count to ten, children know the signage for McDonald's, Burger King, and Dunkin' Donuts (McAlister and Cornwell 2010). I'm in favor of environmental print, and I know the importance of symbolic representation, but I think this phenomenon speaks poorly about our appetites and lifestyles.

Reactions to the obesity epidemic vary in the child care community. I have observed programs that still cling to the 1940s notion that a chubby child is a healthy child. I've also seen programs offer children a slice of apple with a candle in it on their birthdays. Really! The word that comes to my mind is *balance*. Don't we refer to a *well-balanced* diet when discussing healthy eating? What exactly do *well-balanced* and *healthy* mean and to whom? For example, some of us consider a slender or thin figure to be the ideal body type. Some of us view this body type as anorexic and unhealthy. Some of us view a chubby body as a well-fed body; others consider it to be an unhealthy body. Our perception of health can be a class, cultural, and personal issue all at the same time. We need to approach these issues in a mindful way and with an open mind.

We are often too quick to think a child must eat every meal. Too often we cater to children's whims and preferences rather than offering healthy snacks and accepting that if children are truly hungry, they'll eat. It's a fact that children will live without an afternoon snack. It's also a fact that they'll live longer if we insist on healthy, nutritious food on a daily basis. But offering opportunities to share celebrations is also a part of embracing all families in our child care communities.

I'm not a purist. I think an apple slice for a birthday treat is going a little too far! But I've also discovered that celebrations where raw veggies, fruit, cheese cubes, and crackers are served are just as successful as parties where chips and candies are served. Children love bananas, apples, strawberries, and blueberries. They'll often try foods they say they don't like if a cooking activity allows them to prepare food independently. Fruit and veggie taste tests are usually a big success. But let's not go too far—on children's birthdays, let them eat cake!

Questions for Discussion

1. Does your program have nutrition and food-serving policies? What are they based on? Do all families embrace them?

2. How does your center reconcile the expense of healthy food with the budgets of low-income families? How could your program best support these families?

3. Should programs have policies about the use of processed foods, which do not support children's physical development but do support parents' busy lifestyles?

9

Fear of Heights

When I was a child, my family had a huge weeping willow in our backyard. I spent much of my time nestled in the tree's perfect nook, reading book after book. I always felt like I could look out from my nook, but others couldn't look in. Climbing trees was a very big deal when I was growing up. Before the hula hoop was invented, climbing trees was what you did outside when you weren't riding your bike.

When I was a family child care provider in the 1970s, the children would whine because I wouldn't hoist them up into the trees. My rule was, "If you can get up there by yourself, it's probably safe for you to be there." I think this is still a good rule, even though climbing trees have been replaced by climbing structures.

By the 1980s, I was an itinerate educator in schools all over New Hampshire. I loved the rural schools where children had access to small animals, vegetable gardens, and lots of climbing trees. I remember a particular tree at a small-town school. It had to have been three hundred years old. The expansive and numerous branches were low enough that even five- and six-year-olds could enjoy their company. Needless to say, I was horrified when a new administrator from an out-of-state urban district took over and had the tree cut down. She installed a metal climbing structure in its place. "Safety is our first concern," she stated emphatically when I shared my distress. I countered weakly, "Somehow I think children need to feel bark and branches to know they live in a natural world." She went on, "We live in a litigious culture. We can't afford to be sued. I'll take no risks."

My parents taught me to respect authority. It was her school. She needed to do what she thought was right. I left the issue alone. But as I drove home that day, I thought about risk taking. Learning involves taking risks. Growing involves taking risks. It takes skinned knees to learn to roller-skate or ride a bike. We all have a responsibility to keep children safe, but what about the risk of ruling out risks? By the turn of the present century, many commercially made climbing structures became so safe they provided no challenge. The slides barely slant. No wonder the children are always walking up them instead of sliding down them. In addition to the ruled-out-risk slides themselves, many programs have generated a long list of sliding rules:

- Do not walk up.

- Do not slide backward.

- Do not double up.

- Sit on your bottom.

- Slide feet first only.

I think most slides today would be impossible to fall off even if three children, all on their bellies, slid down backward in a train! Again, I'm not suggesting that we should disregard safety. I don't want children playing with fire or knives, but supervised opportunities to take risks might actually help children test their abilities, develop strength and courage, and try something they think they can't manage. This is the way many generations of children have learned how to do things.

Over the years, I've repeatedly heard staff members at large centers malign the "lack of guidance" that other teachers allow on their playground shifts:

- "How can I keep these children safe if the after-school teachers let them hang by one hand from the monkey bars?"

- "Shouldn't we have consistency? We should agree on rules and apply them to all children at all times!"

- "I'm so sick of hearing, 'Karen lets us do it in the afternoon.' I look like the bad guy who doesn't let anybody have fun!"

- "I saw her from the window last week when I was here late for parent conferences. Kids were running up the slide and sliding down the fire pole. She was standing right there and let it happen!"

Let's give serious thought to what really constitutes risk and ask ourselves whether a risk is warranted to nurture growth and development. Climbing to a higher level on a structure is scary the first time, as is sliding down the fire pole, but the fear is followed by elation at accomplishing a new skill and transcending that fear. It's a moment of growth. And just so you don't think I'm against rules, here are some that we use in my program to keep children safe:

- Sneakers (not clogs or open-toed sandals) must be worn for outdoor play.

- Listen to the grown-up in charge. Sometimes different teachers have different rules. That can be okay.

- Rules can change depending on how many teachers and children are outside at a given time.

- Sometimes rules for the same piece of equipment are different because of the age of the children using it.

At my program, we all have varying comfort levels with caution and risk. One educator never lets the children use climbing equipment if she is outside alone. Others let the children use whatever equipment they are interested in, even if they are alone. My cautious colleague has said, "Children could fall and hurt themselves. It makes me nervous." I respect her concerns and her rule that nobody uses the blue climber on her watch. She respects my comfort level and my response, "You're right, someone could get hurt, but that's why we have Band-Aids and insurance." Our rule is to listen to the grown-up in charge.

Safety is a tough issue for a large center to take on. There are so many things to consider. How much risk is too much? How high is too high? If we are too cautious, do we inhibit natural growth and development? How can children conquer a fear of heights if no one lets them try?

Questions for Discussion

1. Does your program have uniform rules regarding safety concerns? Do all staff members consistently carry them out?

2. What are the risks involved in not letting children stretch beyond their gross-motor comfort levels during outdoor play? Generate a list.

3. How should the ages of children, time of day, and teacher–child ratios affect a program's implementation of playground guidelines?

Whatever Floats Your Boat

There is a farm not far from my program where children can pet domestic animals and go on a hayride in a tractor-pulled wagon. The wagon is big enough to allow whole school groups to pile into it. The tour takes riders through fields where autumn offers bright pumpkin patches and spring offers flowers and new vegetables to observe and learn about. The tour guides are quite good and give developmentally appropriate lessons to little ones wanting to explore their world. The farm also has a picnic area with many tables for the visiting school groups. Next to the picnic area is a climbing structure resembling a boat.

Whenever we visit the farm, the children point to the boat, *ooh* and *aah* over it, and want to jump off the wagon the minute they see it. No matter how enticing lunch is or how hungry they are, the children want to play on the boat instead of doing anything else. Once, as the teachers and parent volunteers ate lunch—abandoned by the children, who were playing with delight on the boat—a parent shared that her neighbor had an old boat he'd been trying to sell for years. "Would you be interested in the boat if he'd sell it cheap?" she asked me. I immediately said, "Yes!"

After several weeks of bartering, negotiating, and making transportation arrangements, we had our very own boat sitting in the play yard. On the weekends, my husband does a great deal of work at our school, and he grew up with boats of every kind. The plan to fix and paint the boat to make it "sea worthy" before the next school year brought a twinkle to his eye unlike any other project before it.

Two or three days after the boat was delivered, the facilities manager of my campus called. He asked seriously, if irreverently, "What's with the trash in the backyard?" I laughed and told him, "One man's trash is another woman's treasure!" This was followed by the brief story of the farm field trip; the children's continuing interest in boats, sea creatures, waves, lobsters, fishing, and so on; and our great excitement about the real boat. "Well, we can't have that," he said. This statement was followed by the typical and ever more frequent "litigation nation" talk, which hampers so many attempts to nurture children's interests for real-life experiences.

I was assertive but not aggressive in my response. "Children are growing up in a plastic world," I told him. "I'm not looking for time or assistance from your crew. My family and volunteer families at school are excited about this project. I have all the tools. We know what we need. We will do all the work. I take the children's safety very seriously and would never have purchased the boat if I didn't have a plan for its safe implementation in the play area. We have already purchased lobster nets, fishing rods, toy lobsters and fish, and a remnant of blue indoor-outdoor carpet to use for the 'lake.'" Even as I spoke, I thought of all the Bev Bos inspired play yards I had ever dreamed of and saw it developing for the children in my school.

The children couldn't stop talking about the boat and related topics. One child had a story about fishing with Uncle Joey. Another child said her mom had fixed up an old boat at their camp and that they used it all the time. Another child had been on a Disney cruise and shared that her daddy had called the vessel a "boat," but it seemed more like a skyscraper to her. "It was humongous!" she screeched. Discussing the plans for our boat, Josh noted, "It won't really float. The carpet looks good and all, but it isn't really water; it's just pretend." We supported the children's interest by encouraging them to draw improvements for the boat and the surrounding play area if they wanted to. We also set some of the toy fish and lobsters in the water table with beautiful aqua-colored water and coral to create a place for children to release pent-up excitement about the upcoming project.

In the administration building, however, the perfect storm was brewing. The facilities manager had taken his concerns over my head. I don't know what was said in administration (I admit, I hold a bit of a grudge), but the comments probably went something like this:

- "It's the straw that broke the camel's back!"

- "She just takes things too far!"

- "I was patient about the bird feeders made of pinecones, peanut butter, and birdseed that she placed all over our beautiful blue spruce. Those things attracted rodents. You know, I never saw a bird!"

- "The crew will not be able to mow around the mess she wants to create out there."

- "The neighbors complained about the fort she let the kids build last year."

- "It's really the safety of the children that is at issue here. We can't risk a kid getting hurt."

- "How do we know if her husband knows anything about boats?"

- "This is one big liability!"

- "It's a lawsuit waiting to happen!"

- "My job is to keep this campus free of such dangers."

The following Monday, when I drove into the school parking lot, I was surprised to see that our boat was gone. I drove behind the facilities garage—no boat. I drove behind the auditorium—no boat. Then I drove past the cafeteria Dumpster and saw the boat's front seat and steering wheel peeking out of it. I was furious! I drove back to the parking lot and sat in my car. I was so angry that I couldn't picture myself even going into the center that day.

Everyone who has ever worked for or with me knows how I feel about grown-ups crying at work. When new teachers are hired, cautions are whispered to them in the staff room, "Whatever you do, don't let her see you crying, and never cry in her office when you're upset about something!" This is good information for the staff to pass on about working for me. About crying, I feel like Tom Hank's character in *A League of Their Own* when he shouts, "There's no crying in baseball!" There is no adult crying at the child care center. At the center, crying is reserved for those under the age of eight!

But as I sat in my car—pounding the steering wheel with clenched fists and thinking about the boat's steering wheel sticking out of the Dumpster—angry tears welled up in my eyes. I was glad I was at work early so no one could see my personal meltdown, but the facilities manager must have also arrived early and driven past my car while I was pounding my steering wheel. And he must have known why I was upset, because he was in my office before nine o'clock explaining that the decision was beyond his control and citing lawsuits, liability issues, insurance costs, and his responsibility to our whole system. He said, "I know you guys have wanted a garden out there. How about I go get some nice boxwood and some azaleas? They'll look good from the road, and you'll have your garden!" I knew he was trying. Our campus is small, and we work hard to work well with each other. "Whatever floats your boat, Joe," I said flatly. "I couldn't care less. Do what you want."

Eventually, I sort of got over it, but the boat and its removal is still a topic in our center's culture, and it is brought up when staff get together for celebrations. They call it "Carol's boat" now. When I told the facilities manager, "I couldn't care less," it wasn't true. I did care, and I still do. I mourn for the loss of the real world to children. I mourn for

- scissors that don't cut but are safe;

- hammers that aren't real but are safe;

- plastic tea sets that resemble dishes, sort of;

- dress-up clothes with fake, painted-on stethoscopes coming out of fake, painted-on pockets; and

- knives at the snack table that break before they can cut an apple slice.

And these examples are only the tip of the iceberg. I mourn the natural world lost to children: sticks, stones, weeds, flowers, animals, water, and soil. I mourn the world that forces teachers to use potting soil because the soil from our earth is too dirty. I mourn the world that forces teachers to buy expensive "natural" woodblocks for pretending because real wood from the woodpile might (Oh no!) give someone a splinter.

I remember that old expression from childhood, "Sticks and stones can break your bones, but words can never hurt you." Maybe broken bones are why so many programs cannot bring natural things into the classroom. And even though words have never been certified as a cause of death, when I hear someone say, "Whatever floats your boat," I feel a pain that seems very real to me.

Questions for Discussion

1. Do the staff members at your program agree about what is safe for children and what poses a risk?

2. Are there times when teachers should take a chance and allow children to engage in activities that some people might consider dangerous? Why or why not? Generate a list of hypothetical examples.

3. How do you think children's play in a real boat (adapted for the playground) would differ from their play on a commercial boat-shaped climbing structure?

CURRICULUM

11

The Story on Story Time

It is interesting to me how certain groupings of issues can really get teachers agitated. At a workshop I attended decades ago, present- ers encouraged teachers to reflect on their "flash points" in order to understand their idiosyncratic behavior. That way, educators could get help from colleagues or avoid certain activities with children to improve their teaching. I really loved the workshop, and afterward I spent time thinking about what aspects of working with children and families I find quite manageable and what aspects I find challenging. It was a turning point for me in teaching. It hadn't occurred to me that someone could be a really good teacher of young children without being a fingerpainting enthusiast. It also hadn't occurred to me that a wide variety of interests and abilities is an asset, not a liability, to a staff. Respect and acceptance of our own and others' uniqueness is something most of us need more help with.

Anne Stonehouse (1995, 5–6) counsels us to examine our own prejudices and get them on the table. "Once these issues are out in the open," she says, "questions can be asked about where these views come from. To what extent do they come from our investment in the *correctness* of our own cultural background and lifestyle?" Reflection can help us understand our views about how children should act, what they should eat, where they should sit and stand, and why.

It is common for teachers, for example, to spend a lot of time negotiating how children should behave for story time. Should they be allowed to interrupt or not? Should they be allowed to lie on their bellies? Where should they sit? Should teachers ask questions and encourage discussion throughout the story or hold all talking until the end? More time is spent worrying about these details than on the actual quality of the stories shared, the importance of quality story-telling to overall literacy activities in a classroom, and other serious pedagogical issues. Where children are sitting and what they do with their bodies take up a great deal of time in classrooms for four- and five-year-olds.

Jim Greenman (2005) calls our attention to some of the misguided expectations that exist in full-day programming for young children. Expecting very young children to sit still, stand in line, or even just control their body movement for extended periods is just not fair. Many child care programs, however, operate all day long with behav-ioral expectations that would have been difficult for even the kinder-gartners of many years ago who typically attended programs for only two and a half hours a day.

I have seen good teachers ruin a perfectly delightful story because they interrupt themselves so many times. They tell children to sit up-right, sit crisscross-applesauce, take their fingers out of their noses, get a tissue and wash their hands, keep their feet out of the circle, and so on. With all the interruptions, remembering the story line is hopeless even if you have advanced concentration skills—and four-year-olds don't! I have seen teachers argue passionately with each other because one believes story time should be an option (announced so interested children can gather to hear it) and the other believes story time should be mandatory. Teachers' reasons for their beliefs usually sound some-thing like this:

Teacher 1

- "Next year, these kids won't have a choice. They need to get ready now."

- "Literacy is essential to school success. Painting can be a choice, but not story time."

- "They are too old to lie all over the place to hear stories. They need to sit so everyone can see the pictures."

- "If we let Kevin build with blocks at story time, then half of the boys won't come to story time."

- "The children have so much to learn. Allowing them to choose story time only if the book looks interesting will encourage bad habits."

Teacher 2

- "Why can't they get ready for next year when they get there?"

- "You can enjoy a story just as much on your back or belly as you can on your bottom."

- "I don't see how posture and literacy are so deeply connected."

- "If we select really good books and work hard on our presentation, most of the children will want to come to story time. Besides, it's not like they won't hear you reading if they choose to keep building."

- "The more interested children are, the more they will learn. Over the year, I'll bet everyone will attend story time quite enough!"

There is also the teacher who doesn't connect children's sitting positions or interests with literacy experiences at all. Instead, this teacher focuses on the children's perception of teachers' practices. Her position might sound something like this:

Teacher 3

- "If Sue lets them lie down but Katie and I don't, the children will become detrimentally confused."

- "If teachers can't get their act together, how can we expect the children to?"

- "If we want children to behave at story time or at any other time, we have to provide consistency."

- "If we agree that Kevin needs to be exposed to books about something other than dinosaurs, then we have to support each other in making story time mandatory."

- "The children are going to play us against one other if we don't agree on what we are going to do and how we are going to do it."

I'd be surprised if any early childhood educator has not heard or participated in conversations where similar words have been spoken. I have listened to many teachers in many different programs get very passionate about all of the reasons listed above. In these same programs, however, I have frequently observed the following impediments to effective literacy activities, which no one seemed to be worried about:

- The group size was too large for children to enjoy a meaningful story experience.

- The teachers had not read the book or adequately worked on their presentation.

- The age or ability range of children was too broad, so the book was too sophisticated for some and too boring for others.

- The teachers did not hold the books so that all children could enjoy the illustrations.

- The teachers did not know how to manage relevant questions or mental wanderings during the reading.

Learning to create wonderful experiences with books takes a long time and a good amount of practice. We need to be open to learning from our mistakes, and we need to have the courage to experiment. Watching the children while we read can tell us a great deal; I've seen too many teachers forge on with a story when no one was interested. Maybe the book was a poor choice. Maybe there should have been music and movement before asking the children to sit. Whatever the reason, it's okay now and then to say, "I can see this isn't working." Close the book. Save it for another day. Go outside. Try it again another day with a smaller group. Let the children lie down, ask everyone to sit up, or leave the belly or bottom choice to the children, but do select a book with a great story line, beautiful pictures, and ideas you're excited about sharing with children.

And yet the arguments go on: belly or bum, choice or not?

Questions for Discussion

1. Does your program have stated or unstated protocols for how story time should be presented?

2. Do you think it is important for all teachers in a program to agree on how children and teachers behave during story time? Why or why not?

3. Do you think children can listen to and enjoy a story while they are painting or doing puzzles nearby?

12

Theatrics: How Dramatic Should We Get?

The puppet theater was old but well built. It had a green chalkboard, was made of hardwood, and was purchased from a fine maker of preschool equipment. The veteran teachers at the center had used the puppet theater for twenty years, but some of the newer staff didn't allocate as much time to puppetry as the director wished. Veteran teacher Martha loved to tell and retell her story of Jacob, a child who hardly spoke when he entered preschool but found his voice when he played the troll in a puppet show of *The Three Billy Goats Gruff*. In the safety of the puppet theater, Jacob discovered he could shout, "Who's that tripping over my bridge?"

As in most programs, the teachers had rules governing the use of the puppet theater:

- Only two puppeteers can use the theater at a time.

- The audience must sit behind a line of tape.

- Do not hang on or push at the theater.

And as in most programs, the children sometimes forgot the rules. On one such Wednesday, the puppeteers in charge decided they were comedians. The audience giggled and guffawed until one child crossed the tape line and grabbed at one of the clown puppets. The child holding the puppet jerked it closer to herself. The grabber reached further and, predictably, the theater fell, bumping the heads of two children in the audience. Screams, drama, and chaos took hold for about two minutes. Ice packs and accident reports followed—as did discussion.

The teachers put the puppet theater on the staff-meeting agenda, but the topic took on a life of its own among staff members in the lunchroom:

- "I don't want to be in charge when that thing comes down on a three-year-old and we get sued!"

- "Come on, Brenda, a bump is a bump. It didn't require surgery! Heather's parents weren't even upset, and they are pretty picky."

- "Well, I've heard of people losing their jobs over less."

- "I don't think the school should put us in this position."

- "If we can't afford a newer theater, we should just forget about puppets. Besides, our kids didn't do that well on their phonemic-awareness screening. We ought to spend more time teaching them rather than watching them imitate the Big, Bad Wolf!"

- "I disagree. They learn a lot by doing puppet shows. Remember the story Martha told about the little boy who only started talking when he used puppets?"

- "Oh, right! That was in 1987, you know!"

We have all heard or been a part of conversations that highlight teachers' varying tolerance for risk. In the above example, if the children had been following the rules, the accident would not have happened. The equipment was not the problem. When it comes to accidents, however, people have strong feelings. *Merriam-Webster's Dictionary* (11th ed.) defines *accident* as an "unforeseen and un-planned event." Usually when staff members disagree about an accident, the main point of disagreement has to do with prevention.

We all want to prevent harm to the children in our care; prevention is a serious professional responsibility. We all need to take whatever precautions we can to ensure that our environments for children are free of sharp edges, broken equipment, and toxic elements. The center in question had done all of these things, but the teachers were still divided about the use of the puppet theater. One group believed the following:

- Puppetry is not worth the risk of the theater tipping over and causing harm.

- The center should not expect teachers to use equipment with liability potential.

- Parents should be informed whenever any accident happens at the center.

- Parents should be asked to waive any lawsuits involving accidents beyond staff control.

- The theater is too old and should be replaced by a plastic or resin theater, which would not weigh enough to cause a bump to the head.

- The center should require permission slips from parents before allowing children to participate in puppet play, much like it does before field trips, taking photos, and administering medication.

The other group believed the following:

- Accidents happen.

- Children are supposed to get a few bumps on their way to growing up.

- The administration should talk with families about the risk of not allowing children to take risks. Learning often involves risk.

- In the family handbook, the administration should outline the many steps we take to keep children safe.

- Resin and plastic are not as durable or beautiful in the environment as wood. Just because something is old does not mean it has no value.

- It's ludicrous to get permission slips for the use of puppets. Almost anything could be hurtful if used the wrong way.

For center directors, balancing the various comfort levels of staff members with the basic needs of young children is always a challenge. Balancing individual needs against group needs applies to teachers as well as to children. In this case, the "nays" for keeping the puppet theater outweighed "yeas," so the theater went into the basement storage closet. Many people disagreed with the decision and appealed to the director, claiming that banning puppets was not a developmentally appropriate practice! The director replied that the center was governed by democratic principles and that voting was the only fair way to settle the issue. Many programs or directors would have settled it differently. One of the pro-puppet groups added a humorous note to the staff meeting. She did not like the vote but accepted that a vote was a vote. "Oh, well," she said. "It's like we tell the children, you get what you get, and you don't get upset!"

Questions for Discussion

1. Do you think the group in favor of the puppet theater was being irresponsible?

2. How would this puppet-play dilemma have been settled in your program? How do you know?

3. Do you find diverse attitudes among staff members about how much time should be devoted to math and literacy versus drama, music, and art? How do you handle the differing opinions? Develop a list that informs families about the many ways storytelling, drama, and art contribute to your literacy curriculum.

Literacy

Most teachers would agree that reading quality books to children is a good idea. We know that fairy tales, folktales, and poetry build children's imaginations and vocabulary. The older I get, the more I see Goldilocks as a true hero. She didn't want anything extreme. She wanted things "just right"—not too hot or too cold, not too hard or too soft. For some reason, educators have always struggled with what constitutes "just right" for young children and with who should decide what that is.

In an article for *Exchange*, Lilian Katz (2010) speaks to the importance of nurturing dispositions for learning. By this she means nurturing a love of learning, encouraging inquiry and experimentation, and fostering excitement about ideas. When children experience all of these things, they usually love going to school. Unfortunately, the climate of many schools since No Child Left Behind puts many of these goals at risk. When outcomes and achievement levels are arbitrarily set without consideration to individual learning styles, developmental levels, and language and cultural influences, everyone loses.

Decades ago, Frances Ilg and Louise Bates Ames (1972) cautioned us against setting school- or reading-readiness requirements that expect children to achieve at the same level because they are the same age. One only has to look at a junior high classroom to see the extremes of development within a single chronological age; an assembly of thirteen-year-olds might include a short fellow fingering a matchbox car in his pocket and a five-foot-eleven fellow with fuzz on his chin. Early childhood educators see differences in development when they walk into a room of two-year-olds.

Preschool teachers know that reading and writing successfully require well-tuned fine-motor skills and mastery of eye-hand coordination and left-and-right orientation. Many four-year-olds and some five-year-olds have not yet reached these developmental milestones. When preschool and kindergarten teachers yield to the pressure of preparing children for first grade—which may include forcing four- and five-year-olds to write lowercase letters on lined paper—they risk dampening the positive dispositions for learning that children need to be successful learners. Some children may not only be capable of reading and writing skills, but they may enjoy the process as well. When a system expects all four-year-olds to be writing and to write in a uniform way on prescribed paper, however, we put children at risk of losing their interest in learning and, eventually, of not finishing school.

We often forget that the families we serve rarely have access to the information that we, as early childhood educators, have at our fingertips. Putting information into parents' hands is more important than ever. NAEYC has wonderful short brochures about appropriate curricula, development, and school and learning readiness. These brochures are inexpensive and need to be made available to all our families. As a former elementary educator and preschool-to-public-school transition liaison, I'm well aware that parents frequently assume we always know what we're doing, when, in fact, we are sometimes just as unsure as they are. Kindergarten teachers often have elementary education degrees, which may not have included coursework in young children's growth and development. There are still bachelor's degree programs in elementary education that require coursework in human development but not in child development. We all bring good intentions to work with us, but if we have not been properly prepared to do the job, we are put in an unfair position and so are the recipients of our services.

No Child Left Behind has some worthy goals, such as increasing child outcomes and holding teachers accountable; few of us would argue with the logic of either of these. The implementation of the policy, however, has resulted in sad misunderstandings about these goals and about best practices in early childhood education. Katz (2010) continues to bring our attention back to children's dispositions for learning so that we realize how much is at stake when young children are forced to do only paper-and-pencil work in pre-K and kindergarten classes. At this age, children's primary mode of learning is still through inquiry and gross-motor exploration. The learning is also somewhat egocentric. Early childhood educators know this. The vast majority of parents do not. I was surprised recently by a family-friendly staff person's comments about a mom who was working her child too hard at night to prepare for the district screening for first grade. "You'd think she would know better," the caring but distressed teacher said. "After all, she's an attorney!" I had to remind the teacher that having multiple degrees in engineering, law, or medicine does not give parents as much information about children's growth, development, and needs as a CDA (Child Development Associate) credential, which is usually worth eighteen college credits in early childhood education.

Parents want their children to be successful. They want them to do well in school and to love going there. These are not unreasonable goals. It is our job to show parents why rhyming, clapping, and making patterns is reading readiness in preschool. It's our job to convince them that offering watered-down first-grade curricula to four-year-olds is about as helpful as providing dentures to a gummy, grinning ten-month-old who is late in teething. We don't offer remedial teething classes to children whose mouths blossom later than others. We'd laugh at the ridiculousness of the notion. Remedial reading for children who are not ready to read is just as ludicrous.

This year we initiated the program "I'm Moving, I'm Learning" in our center. The program is full of music children love, exercise that reduces obesity and improves concentration, and concepts that most districts want incoming first graders to know. This year's class is functioning at a level higher than any other year's, a feat that has *not* taken a lot of paper-and-pencil and sit-down work to achieve!

Even after forty years in the early childhood field, I am still pondering which routes are best for nurturing children's growth, intelligence, social skills, and love of learning. I am at a reflective stage in my career. I realize how many mistakes I've made, how many mentors have set me on the right path, how important it is to keep learning, and how important it is to talk about it.

I live in a community for folks over age fifty-five. The condos are nestled among tall pines and hardwoods. We are so close to the city that we have access to most things we want: a music hall, good restaurants, theaters, and even a river for kayaking. It is quiet, convenient, and comfortable. There is one ongoing struggle, however, involving a nearby bridge on which students from a private high school like to spray paint graffiti. My community sends people out to paint over the graffiti, but the kids are back a week later with more paint. How long it takes to cover up the graffiti depends on how acceptable the words and images are for the eyes of the elementary school children whose buses pass under the bridge.

One morning as my husband and I drove under the bridge, I said to him, "I sure hope *Boogr* is someone's nickname. If not, I sure hope the graffiti artist is a freshman." I have gently been told by my husband, my children, my staff, and my students that I almost always have a good point to make when I speak up, but sometimes people have to think hard to make the connections and understand the point. "Do we know someone named Booger?" my husband asked. I recognized his tone as the one he uses when he has no idea what I'm talking about. "Even a freshman should know there's an *e* in *booger*," I said impatiently. Apparently he had not noticed the new graffiti as we drove by. If one of the five-year-olds at school spelled the word *booger* as *bgr*, I would be excited and encouraging, but knowing that high school students (who should know better than to deface public property) can't even spell *booger* right really bothers me.

When I first taught kindergarten in the early 1970s, I used what we called a duplicating machine. The machine had a round drum into which we poured a purple liquid. Teachers turned the machine's handle, and each ditto sheet fell into a tray. We created lined papers for children to practice writing their letters on. Usually the top half had a large letter and a picture of something very basic that began with the letter (*B*, ball), which the children would color. The lower half had lines for printing.

My teaching license was for kindergarten through eighth grade. I had never taken a course in child development. I watched children (usually boys) struggle to color inside the lines. They would grip the crayon too tightly. Often their little tongues would move back and forth over their lower lips as they tried hard, however awkwardly, to please the teacher. We did take a "break" every day to play with blocks or sing, but mostly it was all business. For years after I completed graduate work in early childhood education, I felt guilty about the way I ran my kindergarten classroom in those first several years. I spent way too much time on letter formation, phonics, and prereading skills. I offered too many teacher-directed activities and not enough child choice. I interrupted serious engaged play because it was time for "letter of the week" activities. I knew nothing about child growth and development because this kind of course was not required for my elementary education degree. Everyone did the same thing at the same time regardless of differences in development, learning styles, or interests. But as I drive by that bridge each day, I often think, "Despite the questionable priorities of our early 1970s curriculum, none of those kindergartners, now forty years old, would spell *booger* without the *e!*"

So what should we do about all this? With computer-generated papers due in every college class and spell checkers on every computer, does it matter if no one knows how to spell? Some people, competent and well educated, are highly skilled in many areas but still can't spell. One of my grown children is a high-ranking military officer who flies numerous aircrafts. He also holds a master's degree in business administration. We sent him away to college with *Webster's Misspeller's Dictionary*. He was one of those kids who always looked perplexed when his grandmother told him to look up a word in the dictionary. "If I don't know how to spell it, how can I look it up?" he would ask sincerely. He managed to finish college and graduate school, but he still can't spell. Luckily, he has always had computers or administrative assistants to help him, so he has made a life for himself without this skill that his mother views as essential.

Again, balance is what we need to consider. My son might spell *separate* with one too many *e*'s, but I do know he would never spell *booger* without the *e!* We have a great deal to think about regarding phonemic-awareness screenings, pushed-down elementary curricula in preschools, too many people out of work, parental concerns about children's futures, and the general public's belief that school has some connection to all of these. Thinking is a good start, because mindful reflections on our work will help. Then, as a profession, we need to move past wanting easy answers to realize that we need to be fluid, changing, thoughtful, balanced, and flexible so we can find creative solutions to problems we confront. We may not find a "just right" that would satisfy Goldilocks, but we are sure to do a better job than if we accept the status quo or allow ourselves to continue a pattern that isn't working just because that's the way we've always done it.

Questions for Discussion

1. If school districts expect kindergarten children to show up in September knowing how to make the initial sounds of words, how to write upper- and lowercase letters, and how to read preprimers, should preschool teachers abandon play, artistic expression, and movement to prepare children for the expectations of the following year?

2. Do you and the teachers at your school agree about how to deal with academic pressure on very young children? If not, in what specific ways do you disagree? How do you, as a staff, deal with the disagreements?

3. If you believe that all work in the future will be done on computers, does it matter whether children can use print or cursive or write by hand at all? Why or why not?

Data on Death by Dittos

I f there is one word in our field that brings out as much passion as *day care*, it's *dittos*; I don't know what it is about the *D* words. When I was growing up, I didn't have coloring books because they were expensive (my parents survived the Depression, but they never forgot it). Instead, I colored on brown paper the butcher gave to my grandmother. When my children were young, my mother was thrilled to send them coloring books, which she could finally afford. I had recently earned my graduate degree in early childhood education and thus received these heartfelt gifts with the enthusiasm one might expect if she had sent my children caffeine or nicotine! I hesitated to criticize my mother, but my attitude that coloring books would endanger my children's well-being and rob them of their creativity was apparent. I marvel at my mother's patience with my self-righteousness.

In the 1970s, I read a report called *Not All Little Wagons Are Red: The Exceptional Child's Early Years* (Jordan and Dailey 1973). The report contained stories of children who had been stifled by their teacher's insistence that they color the sky blue, the grass green, and the sun yellow. In those days, we all worried about our attempts to make round pegs fit into square holes, and we believed that doing your own thing was a very honorable enterprise. We were told in college classes and workshops that we should never interfere with a child's creative process. If children asked for help in creating art, we were told not to give them any. A child would ask, "How can I draw a horse?" We would respond with, "What do you think?" and ignore the fact that if the child knew, she wouldn't have asked.

For years, children looked to us for guidance in developing their representational drawings, but we didn't offer any. Later in the 1970s, a colleague of mine took a trip to China to meet with international educators. Teachers from around the world brought samples of art and writing to the seminar. Asian educators looked at drawings from third- and fourth-grade children in the United States and thought they had been done by four-year-olds! My colleague was certain the disparity had to do with the lack of information US children received when they asked teachers for help.

At a NAEYC conference in the 1980s, Professor Bernard Spodek revealed that US children were held from the first grade if they failed to draw fingers on the hands of their self-portrait in their preprimary screening. The administrators interpreted this omission as "help-lessness" when it may have been just an oversight; perhaps the child sneezed and never went back to the hands. A prompting question, such as "How would this fellow catch a ball?" would probably have nudged the child to finish the details. Spodek suggested a variety of ways to work with children on their creative process.

It is true that serious studies of children's drawings indicate certain developmental patterns (Feinburg and Mindness 1994). It is also true that we have a professional responsibility to offer some guidance when children seek our help in creating representational drawings. Questions are a good strategy. Sitting with a child and talking her through the creation of a horse or octopus is often enough. If a child is unhappy with what she produces, we can offer a book and help her make comparisons. We might ask, "How many legs does the horse in the picture have?" Throughout history, artists have used objects to create still lifes. Sculptors have used models. Children need teachers to guide them to the supports they need, and teachers need more extensive training in how to develop the creative process in young children.

I am not suggesting that all trees in children's artwork must have green leaves, as teachers once did. Nor am I suggesting that paper-plate bunnies with precut ears and cotton-ball tails are for everyone. I am saying that we have gone to extremes by avoiding teacher-provided models entirely. This attitude can partially be traced to our teacher education programs, which need to explore art education in a more thorough way. Using a porcelain rabbit as a model for children's interpretive drawings, for example, is very different from hanging twenty identical paper-plate bunnies on a bulletin board. Using a ditto of a frog produced by an enthusiastic parent who knows you are studying them is far more important to your program than discouraging parent participation or, worse, hurting the feelings of the child whose dad drew it!

Every year, the fire department visits our school. They let the children climb on the trucks and blow the horns and sirens. They help the children hold the heavy hoses and shoot water. The firefighters love these visits and are sensitive to the children's needs and fears. At the end of the day, they give each child a hat and a coloring book. The children are ecstatic. Some student teachers, however, are shocked. They tell me their professors would recommend they throw the coloring books away because they set a bad example. I tell them that our classroom has easels, paints, watercolors, pastels, markers, and crayons available every day. Children use playdough, gray clay, and other modeling materials. Frequently, they draw pictures, paint paintings, and make pottery. And the day the fire department comes, they use coloring books!

Questions for Discussion

1. Judy, a preschool teacher, is studying winter birds with the five-year-olds in her class. She sets out red and brown paint and feathers and encourages the children to make cardinals, which they've observed at their bird feeder. Emma's mom says Emma was sad that her bird had to be red. She wanted hers to be green. If you were Judy, how would you respond?

2. How does creativity develop in young children? What are some strategies for nurturing it?

3. Has your early childhood education degree adequately prepared you to raise young children's aesthetic awareness? Do you know how to elicit their artistic expression?

To Use or Not to Use:
Technology Is the Question!

I still remember the horror I felt twenty-five years ago when I walked into a child care center and observed twenty four- and five-year-olds sitting on little chairs watching Bugs Bunny cartoons! The characters on the screen were pushing, hitting, and cracking vases over one another's heads, actions typical of cartoons in those days. I was appalled. It was not unusual at the time for large child care programs to use television to keep children quiet. Those of us in educational circles, however, frowned on this practice. Plus, I was at this center to supervise student teachers, so I was surprised that the college had approved this setting.

Television captured everyone's time and interest so quickly, and it was a concern for educators and a problem for children long before anyone even thought of monitoring it. Eventually, an extensive body of research documented the relationship between viewed violence and actions in the play yard (Carlsson-Paige and Levin 1990). Researchers also traced children's emotional reactions and nightmares to viewing graphic violence on screen. Many quality programs for young children immediately responded to this research by banning the use of screen media entirely. Banning screen media is another example of educators taking a good idea—sparing children the trauma of viewing graphic violence—too far. It is the abuse, not the use, of media that hurts children.

My favorite week of school is the week before we close for the winter holidays. The teachers have a *Polar Express* train for our train table.

We read the book of the same name by Chris Van Allsburg over and over again as children quietly hang on every word. On one of the days, the children and teachers wear their pajamas to school. We watch the *Polar Express* movie from start to finish, lying on the floor in our PJs, drinking mugs of hot cocoa, and munching on popcorn. As the film draws to a close, the teachers tiptoe through the group and place a sparkling sleigh bell hanging on a red ribbon around each child's neck. Like the movie, the experience is magical!

Today we are fortunate to have scrupulously prepared DVDs of award-winning children's books, such as *The Velveteen Rabbit*, *Charlotte's Web*, and *The Snowman*. For school-age children, there are wonderful PBS programs, such as *Anne of Green Gables* and *Anne of Avonlea*. National Geographic films are beautifully made and allow us to share arctic, rain forest, and desert ecosystems. The American Girl DVDs offer appealing programming based on history. Likewise, there are high-quality, appropriate computer programs and Internet sites for children of all ages.

I think about the programs that have children in their care for more than ten hours a day. It seems valid for teachers and children to relax late in the day by watching *Sesame Street* or other *appropriate* programming every now and then. It provides a little bit of home for children who spend eleven hours a day in child care.

Howard Gardner reminds us that there are many kinds of intelligence. For some children, watching *Owl Moon* is a more engaging experience than listening to it. Using multiple approaches means everyone can engage. Many children love the captivating book *Stranger in the Woods* by Carl R. Sams II and Jean Stoick. Viewing the movie is a way to extend the story. I love seeing the wonder and delight in preschool children's eyes when they see a favorite story come to life in a movie.

Early childhood educators need to learn how much technology to use in their classrooms and when to use it. Certainly the same rule of thumb we use with books applies: never use something with children that you have not previewed. Carefully select on-screen activities to offer children a rich, high-quality experience. Talk about on-screen content the same way you discuss books. Don't allow yourself to use screen time as a backup for every time the going gets rough, but don't be afraid to find a favorite DVD when the weather has prevented you from going outside for four days in a row and the children and staff are tired and cranky. Snuggle into big cushions, turn down the lights, adjust the indoor temperature, and don't forget the hot chocolate (or lemonade, if it's hot outside)!

Questions for Discussion

1. How do movies of award-winning books support Howard Gardner's theory of multiple intelligences?

2. Is it ethical for teachers to use developmentally appropriate screen-time activities to cope with children's poor behavior, a long period of inclement weather, or staff illnesses (creating higher teacher–child ratios than all are used to)? Why or why not?

3. What media-use policies can be established to prevent the abuse of media?

REGULATION

Child Care Licensing:
Friend or Foe?

I was recently at a meeting for child care center directors, and the topic of licensing came up. The immediate response to the topic was groaning. Fortunately, my state's Department of Health and Human Services takes child care very seriously—and has for many years—so I'm always a bit put off when I hear the groaning and whining.

Our child care bureau holds hearings in every corner of the state and listens to provider input prior to revising regulations. Many changes to our regulations are the direct result of provider input. Here are a few examples:

- Naptime ratios have been adapted to support staff planning.

- Temperature restrictions regarding outdoor play have been eliminated.

- Special exception procedures have been instituted to support families or programs in crisis.

The last time my state's regulations were revised, I got really cranky. I overheard staff-room chitchat about the number of changes being made, the amount of money it was going to cost, and how impossible and unfair it was going to be. As a supervisor in the building, I was uncomfortable with the tone of most of this chitchat. "It sounds like you went to the public hearing last week," I said to three teachers discussing the changes. "Well, not exactly," one spoke up, "but my sister-in-law's mother's next-door neighbor is a family child care provider, and one of the people in her provider group went to the hearing, so we got all the information from her." This teacher did not recognize how closely the flow of information resembled a game of "telephone," an activity where a group of people pass a message around a circle and giggle when they see how the words change from the first person to the last. I received more than a few frowns from colleagues when I started calling these public hearings "show up or shut up" events. Irreverent as it sounds, there is something to be said for having your facts straight before offering your opinions. If you don't take time to participate, then surrender your right to pontificate!

Many years ago, I participated in Head Start management training. The instructor encouraged every Head Start manager to carefully and frequently read the performance standards that directed our practice. She added that memorizing them, if possible, would be even more desirable. Questioning glances darted around the room. Finally, someone spoke up. "Isn't that overdoing it? If we have the standards in writing on our desks, we can consult them quickly if we have a question." The instructor acknowledged that a desktop reference was a great idea but went on to say that most of us would also work in the field with teachers who had been working in Head Start for ten or more years. The instructor had spent the last twenty-five years of her career at Head Start and shared with us the "epic mythology" regarding the Head Start performance standards. She said we'd hear arguments in staff rooms and classrooms that end with someone saying, "Besides, it's in the performance standards." She cautioned us that half the time it would not be there. "Carry a copy with you at all times," she suggested. "When it comes up, say, 'Show me the page!'"

I find educators' recollections of specific state licensing regulations to be similar. I have heard teachers quote regulations when they want a particular action. Then, upon inquiry, they find that the regulation was true in the state where they used to work but not in New Hampshire. Usually, when a teacher confidently quotes licensing regulations, other teachers don't question her because they aren't informed enough themselves!

Some licensing regulations have a subjective quality. I directed a program many years ago that was located on three and a half acres of land near a very busy highway. About an acre of the land was fenced in to provide children with abundant outdoor play spaces. Inside this fenced area was another small fenced area where wading pools were set up in the summer. In October, hurricane-force winds blew off the gate of the pool-area fence. We set the gate aside, planning to fix it in the spring. After a February licensing visit, we were written up as follows: "Gate to fenced area is off its hinges and resting against the building." I felt low-level annoyance at the wording. If the word *swimming* had been added in front of the word *area*, I would have been fine with it. Every child care professional in New Hampshire would have known what it meant.

Unfortunately, while this was still on record, a local newspaper ran a story about licensing violations in local child care programs. My broken gate made the news. Because of the absence of the word *swimming* and because I was president of the New Hampshire AEYC at the time, colleagues mentioned it in horror. "You must be so embarrassed," was the most frequent comment. I replied, "Well, yes. It was a shame they omitted the word *swimming*." Immediately people said, "Oh! It was only the fence to your swimming area. Good grief, it was February in New Hampshire!" I never complained. The program was a strong one. I didn't give the article much thought. If I lived in Florida, however, the entire scenario would have been different.

The variables that affect the implementation of licensing regulations nationwide are many. They include climate, traffic patterns, location, ages and number of children, ages and training of caregivers, cultural expectations, and whether a setting is urban or rural, just to name a few. Several years ago, for example, I faced a cultural dilemma when new refugee families wanted their little ones to sleep in the same crib. I believe, as a program director, I have a huge responsibility to follow state regulations carefully to set an example for the staff. I also have a huge responsibility to respect and honor the wishes of families for the care of their children. So what is a director to do? I called the licensing bureau and was told I could file for an exception. I was told the same thing last year when a mother of three children under age four requested that her three-year-old daughter be allowed to begin our program after the winter holidays. We were licensed for children ages four to seven. This mother was expecting her fourth child in February and didn't want her daughter to have to adjust to a new child care center and a new baby at the same time. Her daughter would turn four just two weeks after starting care with us.

The child care bureau asked me to explain the situation in writing and to post a notice to enrolled families in a visible place, telling them about this one-time-only special exception. It took a tiny bit of time and made the families and their children much more comfortable. There was no red tape, hassling, or problem. I have consistently found licensing professionals to be colleagues who, like early childhood educators, spend their days trying to promote quality care and education for children and their families. Even so, I hear as much negative "them versus us" chatter about licensing professionals as I hear about parents and families. Both make me uncomfortable. If we are not part of the solution, we are part of the problem.

At a recent meeting, I heard several providers share their angst about the recent focus of licensing professionals at our center. They asked each other, "How can that suddenly be a violation when we've all done it for years?" I reminded them of the dangerous way we used to transport infants from the hospital fifty years ago. We sat in the front seat of the car, holding our infants in our arms. Life and culture have changed a lot since then, and several variables affected this change in transportation practice:

- Seat belts and infant car seats did not exist at the time.

- There were fewer vehicles on the roads fifty years ago.

- Cars did not go as fast.

- Women often gave birth in local community hospitals, which meant moms and babies didn't have to travel far to get home.

Few of us would debate the improvements in cars, infant car seats, roads, and medical facilities that we now take for granted. This is the face of progress.

It would be foolish, with regard to regulations on peanut allergies, for providers to say, "Well that's just absurd. Kids love peanut butter. I've been a provider for twenty years. I've always served peanut butter, and I'm not about to change now because of all this allergy hoopla!" We know that peanut allergies were not as prevalent twenty years ago. About sunblock use, it would be foolish for providers to say, "I grew up on the water. We never used sunblock. We used to mix iodine and baby oil to enhance our tan!" We also knew nothing of the ravages of skin cancer at the time.

To make things more complicated for licensing professionals, rules regarding things like insect repellant, sunblock, and outdoor play temperatures are all dependent on geographic conditions, which change from region to region. It is the job of a child care licensing unit to assess the needs of children, families, and facilities in the context of safety, economics, culture, geography, and progress. It is not an easy line of work. When licensing professionals and providers do not engage in open, honest, and respectful communication, we take focus away from the goal of both of our professions: to support young children and their families in care and education settings.

We need to appreciate the women and men who spend their careers in child care licensing positions, as they have an often thankless job. Like the rest of us, they make errors in judgment from time to time, but generally they spend their work life trying to ensure the health and safety of young children in child care. Our collaboration and cooperation with licensing professionals is critical to our child care communities.

In addition to writing the child care bureau for special exceptions or to complain, how about sending a thank-you note?

Questions for Discussion

1. What is the relationship between licensing professionals and child care providers in your state?

2. Are you well informed about the child care regulations in your state? Why or why not?

3. Do you think providers make assumptions about regulations and the reasons for them? Do these assumptions prevent providers from clarifying rules with their licensing contacts? Give examples.

Accidents Happen

My daughter's finger was broken in child care when she was four years old. I was glad. That must sound perverse, but let me explain.

I was the executive director of the center at the time. I already knew that four-year-olds often don't understand the scientific properties of a stone versus a sponge. When a child reaches for a dolphin or whale in the water table, another child using the water table might pounce at the reaching hand with whatever happens to be in his. In this case, the "whatever" was a good-sized stone that gave a natural look to the seascape. Bam! Screams! Tears! Ice! Twenty minutes after the incident, the finger was getting larger, not smaller, so we went to the emergency room.

I didn't have to explain the scenario to myself. I already knew how and why it happened. I didn't have to say to anyone, "These are very young children, and there was an absence of malice. No, I'm sorry. I can't give you the other child's name." I didn't blame the other child. He was four. The experience never changed my daughter's friendship with the boy or her love of the water table. And because I was my own supervisor at the time, I had no explanations to give to a manager. I didn't lose sleep wondering how it would all end. It was fairly simple. Perhaps the most difficult thing was that my daughter couldn't play in the water table for a couple of weeks because of the splint.

The story would have been very different, however, if the child had been someone else's. At the very least, it would have been stressful to inform the child's family of the broken finger and to explain that the other child was just acting like a typical four-year-old. Depending on the parents' response, there could have been fear of a lawsuit.

For at least twenty years, litigation hysteria has been prevalent in our field, but only recently have we started talking about it out loud. Our professional journals have even started carrying articles about the risk of raising children in antiseptic environments. Still, most of us are pretty uncomfortable with many scenarios, and we are unsure of the right direction to take. It is not a figment of my imagination that teachers have risk, caution, and political correctness—rather than developmentally appropriate practice—on their minds a great deal. To make matters worse, educators are often afraid to air their fears with other colleagues.

Taking risks is an essential part of learning and growing. I understand the need for caution when caring for other people's children, and I understand that many educators have no control over playground or woodworking-bench policies. I know that some projects can be successfully undertaken in homes with two or three children but simply cannot not be implemented in group care. But I also know that the word *accident* implies an absence of malice. Children trip over their own feet and break bones. Children fall down several steps and are perfectly fine. We cannot always predict or prevent these curious mishaps we call accidents. That's why they are called accidents.

So how do we strike an appropriate balance? It is no easy task, but a proactive stance is far superior to a reactive one. Just as our field suggests we should talk to parent groups about toddler biting, we need to develop plans with parents for balancing risk and caution:

1. Have a family meeting to discuss accidents.

2. Gather stories from parents about accidents that happen at home.

3. Get parents talking with each other about the amount of risk and caution they are comfortable with.

4. Have parents and staff members work together on safety policies for the program.

5. Talk about individual differences and how they might be accommodated.

6. Live with new policy guidelines for a few months, and then revisit them in another family meeting. Does anything need to be adjusted?

In addition to the above, center administrators might take time to reflect on the rights of individual children and the rights of the group. It is possible for us to allow many children to participate in an activity while others engage in something else. For example, if educators plan to make s'mores during a unit on camping, the few children whose parents don't want their children near a campfire can gather twigs for the fire or prepare the picnic table for snacktime. Creating policies to accommodate one or two parental reservations may not always be necessary.

We all want easy answers to hard questions, but when it comes to honoring children, families, best practices, diversity, cultural pluralism, parental wishes, and individual differences in children, striking a balance may be the best we can do. That and remembering you can never please all of the people all of the time!

Questions for Discussion

1. Do you think your center's policies on risk should be more rigorous or more relaxed? Why or why not?

2. Are there activities at your program that make you nervous? What are they? How are they handled? How would you prefer to see them handled?

3. Do you think different teachers should be allowed to have different policies with children based on their own comfort with risk? Why or why not?

18

The Numbers Don't Lie, or Do They?

The neighborhood where I grew up was full of O'Haras and Murphys and Mulligans. As a child, it never occurred to me that it was an ethnic neighborhood. It was a different time. Small families in my neighborhood had five or six children, and large families had fourteen. The average was about ten. It didn't occur to me or the other children that we were not getting enough attention. Our life was all we knew. This kind of childhood certainly had its benefits: Most of us learned to get along with people of all ages. All girls—as I said, it was a different time!—could change a (cloth) diaper by age twelve. We did not expect rooms of our own, privacy, or window seats in the car. Sharing was a way of life and a necessity.

This experience, however, did not prepare me to be a child care director for early childhood educators who watch teacher–child ratios like hawks. It has always been a challenge for child care directors to determine which comes first, the teacher or the enrollment. Unfortunately, few programs have the financial luxury of hiring teachers at worthy wages to sit and wait while a class fills.

In graduate school in the 1970s, I viewed a film that exposed how much waiting very young children were expected to do in a typical US primary school, in part because of high enrollment. At the time, baby boomers were filling up the new suburban elementary schools beyond capacity at a record pace. In this huge swell of public-education enrollment, class sizes often went beyond thirty-five, and many children fell through the cracks. These children were done a disservice. If you were ahead of or behind the group in any way, it was your poor luck. Lots of children hated school or found it boring, which in retrospect makes a lot of sense. The film made the point that six- and seven-year-old children quickly feel lost without adequate adult guidance.

In the past two decades, dramatic changes to the overcrowded conditions have occurred (in early childhood care, that is, not necessarily in public schools). Accredited child care centers led the movement for appropriate teacher–child ratios and group size in early childhood programs. When it comes to ratios in child care, however, problems in numbers can easily arise. I have never envied my colleagues in child care licensing, who have to determine appropriate ratios and group size, because child care is so unpredictable. Trends in enrollment—and almost everything else in child care—change faster than fashion for tweenage girls!

Unfortunately, in our attempts to keep teacher–child ratios stable so children don't have to wait for long, unmanageable periods, some of us have started to believe that children shouldn't have to wait at all. This attitude is not helpful for building prosocial skills in preschoolers, because few people can have exactly what they want when they want it every time. In her article "Self-Esteem and Narcissism: Implications for Practice," Lilian Katz (1993) challenges us to explore the inadvertent ways we encourage young children to focus on themselves rather than others. Preventing children from ever having to wait might be one of these ways; I think this is another huge, and related, issue for our field. We need to get back to a comfort level that allows us to say no to children when an activity is too involved for the number of children and teachers. For example, you might say, "That was so much fun last week, but I'm the only teacher today, and it would be too hard to do that without help."

We know that the quality of child care in the United States is strongly related to both adult–child ratios and group size (Travers et al. 1980). We need to take that fact seriously. At the same time, early childhood programs in other countries that have both larger group sizes and higher adult–child ratios also function quite well. This tells us that there must be sociocultural factors that make large-group care of young children work.

I have had wonderful days with large groups of children. Sometimes when a teacher is out and there is no substitute teacher to be had, I've had serious talks with children about my need for their cooperation because I'm alone. I shift a few things around and have a better than average day. I've also had days when the group is smaller than usual. Even with two teachers and a volunteer to help with the small group, I've needed ibuprofen before noon. On these days, whining might be contagious and activities less engaging than I'd hoped. Everyone might be out of sorts. Children might erupt into unprovoked tantrums. Everyone might be miserable, even if no one quite knows why.

As a director, I have documented attendance rates for years. I have noticed a pattern that many other directors tell me is true for them as well. The pattern resembles the business formula that it takes nine positive comments about a company to make up for one negative review. I find that most teachers happily manage their low-enrollment (or low-attendance) groups for weeks at a time with little comment, but if they have one afternoon of full enrollment (or—oh no!—one child above capacity), the day hangs in staff-room conversation for two weeks. I often ask my staff to guess at the month's average daily attendance. They consistently report numbers in excess of the actual numbers. They say, "Fourteen children is nothing. Last summer, I was alone most days with sixteen children." When attendance figures were tracked, this teacher was alone with sixteen children for only two days of the entire summer—and she was only alone on those days for two hours. I'll admit that ten minutes can feel like two hours if a staff person is alone with six or eight five-year-olds on a rainy day, but, overall, it's not as bad as most teachers seem to think. High-enrollment days just take on a life of their own in an educator's memory!

I suggest we look at the issue of ratios—as well as any other issue in early childhood care—from a variety of angles. Safety is a huge factor when pondering numbers. For instance, more attention to ratios is required during swimming, sledding, and field trips than at naptime. My state makes regulation accommodations for all of these scenarios. It's important for us to admit, however, that sometimes we can be overwhelmed by a single child, depending on his or her behavior. In these cases, it doesn't matter if we are alone with two children or six—it's hard!

As a director, I'm always concerned about teachers establishing their comfort levels at times when a classroom is under ratio. When the class is finally at full enrollment, these teachers feel they need an aide. To prevent this phenomenon, I encourage one of the teachers in a room to work on planning, organizing, or anything else that needs to be done when the classroom number is low. That way neither the children nor the teachers set an unrealistic comfort level. Veteran teachers are quick to admit that too many adults in a room can be as problematic as too few. Often when student teachers, volunteers, and special-education teachers arrive on the same day, chaos ensues.

Too many programs violate ratio policies because the economic conditions for child care have become so austere. Children deserve better. At the same time, programs that adhere too strictly to the letter of the law are going under. Again, children and families deserve better. The same questions need to be asked every day—and sometimes many times in one day:

- Who is here?

- What activities are planned?

- Are children and staff members comfortable?

Many teachers look at enrollment numbers when planning group size. It is an industry-based fact that full attendance is not the norm. Many programs (often those who take professionalism most seriously) are forced to close because directors have not managed the numbers. We need to look at this problem more seriously. I have seen staff members complain, whine, or feign concern for their coworkers about these issues: "I stayed late because she was over regulation."

Each year, my state's licensing bureau gives child care programs twenty "get out of jail free" days. If we know we'll be over our numbers, we can call and tell them. I once supervised a teacher who watched teacher–child ratios like a hawk and reported her peers whenever they were over ratio. She reported teachers no matter the situation, even when they were over by only one child for only a short period. After one such incident, I called the state to inquire whether I needed to use one of the twenty "get out of jail free" days if an extra child was only throwing off numbers for an hour. The licensor very appropriately suggested using common sense and discretion. This didn't change much in the attitude or behavior of the ratio-focused young teacher; she continued to use the numbers talk to erode staff morale. Other directors tell me this is common in their programs too.

We need to reflect on our behaviors to determine where our motivation lies. Is being over ratio really a safety issue in this situation? How can we best manage the group of children? What kinds of strategies will make conditions optimal for both staff and children? Do we want to make things work? Or do we just want to whine? If a teacher is alone in the classroom and an emergency occurs, she can call 911. Each staff member at our center always has a cell phone in his or her pocket.

Returning to that neighborhood I grew up in (granted in less complicated times), my aunt used to leave her six children with my mom, who also took care of her own five children and our neighbor's four children. My mom was in charge of fifteen of us, ranging in age from two to fourteen. She didn't have an aide! We knew we had to cooperate. Older kids helped younger ones. "Don't let your brother fall into the creek," Mom would say as we headed out to pick strawberries or wildflowers. One time my brother fell off his bike and broke his arm. That was tough because we had no car, but the large group of older kids organized and got help from a neighbor. My brother got a cast. We all signed it. Grandma used to say, "If children are going to do interesting things, there will always be a bump or two along the way." Ah, those were the days.

Questions for Discussion

1. How many children are too many children? Who decides? What factors create danger and are unacceptable?

2. What variables informed your answer to the previous question, how many children are too many children? Can a single decision account for the various circumstances that might arise in a typical child care day? Why or why not?

3. Does multiage grouping call for ratios to be lower or higher? Why? What factors should affect guidelines for multiage classrooms?

19

First Do No Harm

Health and safety are usually at the top of our priority list for children, but when it comes to articulating what it means to keep children healthy and safe, we often find ourselves at a loss for words. Other times, we have too many words that are all in conflict.

A report from the Center on the Developing Child at Harvard University (2010, 2) includes this statement about health: "Health is more than merely the absence of disease—it is an evolving human resource that helps children and adults adapt to the challenges of everyday life, resist infections, cope with adversity, feel a sense of personal well-being, and interact with their surroundings in ways that promote successful development." Good health involves comprehensive mental and physical wellness, not just the absence of negative factors.

In "Places for Childhood in the Twenty-First Century: A Conceptual Framework," Jim Greenman (2005, 7) writes the following: "The drive to protect our children is profound and easily can lead to cleansing their lives of challenge and depth. Early childhood is a time when children begin to live in the world and hopefully learn to love the world. They can't do this when fenced off from the messy richness of life to live in a world of fluorescent lights and plastic toys, two-dimensional glowing screens, and narrow teaching instruction. Scrubbing and polishing raw experience in the name of health and safety scrapes away the natural luster and meaning of childhood." Many of us have seen the impact of focusing too strongly on the letter of the law rather than our program goals. This tendency usually ends with diminished experiences robbed of their essence, as Greenman describes.

Margie Carter references Greenman's perspective in a discussion of core values. Like Greenman, she believes too many programs get caught in letter-of-the-law thinking, which distracts them from living and implementing the core values they print on their brochures. Carter (2010, 18) writes, "Programs are managed with a primary focus on licensing regulations, risk management, and budget constraints. What stands out for me is how easily this limited focus results in mediocre quality for children and families and minimal job satisfaction for staff." I've frequently observed the misdirected focus that Carter describes, and it dampens the energy and morale of good staff members.

This past year at my program, the use of sunblock became an issue. Our program usually has adult–child ratios most programs only dream of. At the end of the day, however—in the hours before many children are picked up and after morning staff members have gone home—one teacher truly has her hands full. Sleep mats are being put away, children are ready for afternoon snack, school-age children are arriving, and other children are using the bathroom and preparing to go outside.

All summer, teachers applied sunblock on the children before going outside, both in the morning and afternoon. That fall, a new afternoon teacher came into my office and asked me if she really needed to apply sunblock after three o'clock in the New England autumn; the afternoon was hectic enough as it was. I looked in my licensing regulations manual and could not find a definitive statement on sunblock use. Teachers had strong and varied opinions about this issue, so I called my licensing professional, who said, "Common sense needs to dictate. Have the children wear hats and light shirts." She told me she'd had complaints from parents about sunblock use, both from those whose children had been sunburned and from those who didn't want any product they didn't pick out themselves applied on their children. This serious licensing professional reminded me, "You'll never please all of the people all of the time." I decided to leave the center's policy on sunblock use to the discretion of individual teachers.

I appreciated being given the freedom to follow the spirit of the law, rather than just the letter of the law.

I have found in my many years of experience, however, that some teachers just don't want things left to their individual discretion. I'm not sure why this is, but there are probably multiple causes:

- It's more fun to bicker.

- We'd rather worry and complain about how other people spend their time than enjoy the freedom to do things our own way.

- We don't want to be responsible for our choices. What if they don't go as planned?

- It's easier if someone else has to make the choices.

- If we aren't successful, we can say it's because we were forced to do it "her" way.

- Being right is more important than doing things efficiently.

- We are so used to doing things one way that we don't want the hassle of breaking a habit.

Margie Carter (2010) is right when she says that staff morale suffers when too much focus is given to mechanics and not enough to creativity, flexibility, and trying things differently. I see it frequently in my own workplace. We often get caught in the trap of thinking things must be done a certain way, forgetting that we made the rules in the first place.

For example, I work in a fairly small program, and we all eat lunch together. Some children, just like some foods, do not mix well. The same child who plays well with others during center, music, and outdoor times may not be a good partner at the lunch table, for whatever reason. Staff members have also long complained that lunch takes too long. A few of us believe that some children slow down others at lunchtime. They either talk too much instead of eating or laugh at what others are eating, causing tears that require time-consuming interventions. At a staff meeting, a colleague suggested we assign seats to children at lunch to see if it would streamline the process. The same teachers who frequently complained about the transition from lunchtime to naptime were up in arms at this suggestion! How could we even think about telling the children where to sit at lunch? Didn't this limit opportunities for children to develop social-emotional skills? Wasn't this a violation of individual freedom? Wouldn't this prevent spontaneous friendships and lunchtime partners? The colleague, a sensible woman with decades of experience, said she was not trying to violate anyone's personal freedom. She was only trying to improve the timeline for cleaning tables and vacuuming so we could set out sleep mats earlier. "Isn't that what you guys have been upset about for weeks?" she asked. The other teachers stammered, "Well, yes, but not at the price of assigned seats!"

Thinking of children's health and well-being as an "evolving human resource," as the Harvard report suggests, is an exciting perspective if we think of *evolving* as a process of continuous change and adaptation. Good health should be an evolving human resource for all of us. Stress and ill health in early childhood programs can come from refusing to evolve in any area—for example, those related to new licensing regulations, accreditation rules, or scientific research. Refusing to evolve could mean being so tied to institutional memory that we find ourselves saying, "We do it this way here," instead of asking, "Why do we do it this way? Let's think more about it." In the lunchtime example, maybe assigned seats are a good option if it means teachers are more relaxed and less stressed during the transition to naptime; less stressed teachers might mean less stressed children. If nothing else, it's worth trying out for a few weeks to see what happens.

Looking at another example, teachers frequently get on each other's nerves regarding the routine use of materials. Every preschool has manipulative materials. Like fingerpaint, it's hard to picture a preschool without them. The variety and quantity of manipulatives often depends on the budget, but most of us have Lego blocks, Unifix cubes, and wooden geometric shapes, among others. The use of manipulatives in dramatic play has become a staff issue at every program I've ever been associated with. I know a teacher named Renee who loves providing math activities for young children. She excels at finding creative ways for children to use the materials and to think about them in serious ways. I know I would be better with numbers if I'd had a kindergarten teacher like her. She organizes the manipulative area and knows the location of every Cuisenaire rod in our building.

Her coteacher, Marcus, is equally as gifted in facilitating dramatic play. One morning after he read *Stone Soup*, an enthusiastic group of four-year-olds headed for the dramatic-play area to fetch every pot in the room. The orange and green Unifix cubes went into the pots, acting as the carrots, peas, and beans of the soup. "Corn!" the children shouted as they threw in the yellow cubes. The children were mixing pretend soup, practicing language skills, and reenacting the story line. It all looked good to me. I observed Marcus's pleasure at seeing the children's excitement flow from the story into free play. Then I caught a glimpse of Renee heading into her office for planning time. There was a tension in her back and face that I was unaccustomed to seeing, but I didn't give it much thought at first. Later in the day, I noticed someone had written "appropriate use of materials" on the clipboard where we jot ideas for staff-meeting topics. I realized there was a connection between Renee's tension, *Stone Soup*, and the Unifix cubes.

Whether we are talking about health and safety or the use of materials, introducing an element of mindfulness to our work can help, as can honestly discussing our differences. If we think about the idea from the Harvard report, "Health is more than the absence of disease," we might notice that it applies to curricula and communication as well. By using our evolving human resources to bring the most we can to the children in our programs, we can promote their successful development, help them use their skills, and teach them how to cope with adversity.

We keep trying. We talk and reflect and read and think, but sometimes we still can't quite leave things to the individual discretion of classroom teachers. But at least we ask ourselves "Why?" more than we used to—and that's a good thing!

Questions for Discussion

1. Do teachers at your program always agree on how materials should be used? What do you do when you don't agree?

2. Do you think there is a tendency in our field to focus more on the letter of the law than the spirit of the law? Why or why not?

3. Do you think all of the teachers in your program could agree on the appropriateness of using Unifix cubes for vegetables in dramatic play? Are there similar issues where debate would ensue?

20

How High Do We Reach?

In the training video *Thinking Big: Extending Emergent Curriculum Projects* (Carter, Felstiner, and Pelo 1999), Ann Pelo and Sarah Felstiner share stories about their own personal growth as teachers. They discuss their journey from wanting to keep children entertained and under control to realizing the benefits of offering children long periods to explore their own ideas in ways that make sense to them. In the video, the teachers describe how much more everyone learned when more time and thought were given to daily activities.

In early childhood education, we talk a lot about diversity and respect, but when it gets down to finding practices that make sense for all of us, we often lose patience with each other. We all want to keep children healthy, clean, safe, and content, but we don't always agree on the components that make this happen. Recently, a teacher in Massachusetts used dirt from her yard for a classroom experiment with worms and planting. Afterward, she was told by her school principal that she could only use bagged potting soil with the children because dirt was, well, too dirty! We don't always need mindless policies to prevent us from doing our best work—we sometimes get in our own way.

Carter, Felstiner, and Pelo's training video points out how teachers bring ideas from their college work or nonacademic experiences and hold them as mandates for how things ought to be done. As the teachers in the video work together, observe the children, and discuss their observations, they realize much of what they've always done wasn't necessary for children's well-being. All of us agree, for example, that hand washing is important in preventing the spread of germs. Some of us think soap and warm water will do the job. Others argue with administrators about the specific ingredients in the soap and think using a thermometer to ensure the exact water temperature is necessary. Some of us think children have increasing sensitivity to a variety of things because our lives have become too antiseptic. Others think the world is harboring too many toxins; children shouldn't be allowed to interact with substances in the air, water, and dirt (previously thought to be safe) unless they are sanitized, thus the ban on natural dirt.

In the case of Pelo and Felstiner, the issue of safety became paramount in a study of heights. In her teacher training, Felstiner had learned that children's block structures should not be higher than their shoulders for safety reasons. She and Pelo discussed the children's interest in heights and decided to take a field trip to a hardware store to purchase a safe, untippable stepstool for making higher structures.

This reminded me of my friend Susan's visit to Reggio Emilia. She described the experience as life and pedagogy altering, as many of us do on our first visit to the early childhood programs in northern Italy. During her tour, she saw children standing on tabletops to finish their block structures. The children worked independently as adults walked through the building and provided encouragement and support. The adults never said, "Get off the table. It's not safe." Susan told me how surprised she was to see toddlers eating from china plates. "The real difference," she said, "was in the way the Italians trust children to manage themselves and their work. They believe that even babies will treat beautiful things with care. They don't think adults always have to be in charge: policing, directing, and interfering. I saw a lot of things you'd never see here, but I didn't see any accidents."

When we trust children to work well, to stay safe, and to learn from their mistakes and successes, and when we provide them the freedom and time to pursue engaging play and projects, our trust is usually rewarded. Teachers in the United States are not used to thinking this way. Just as Pelo and Felstiner discovered, moving from fear and control to trust is a journey. Taking risks, collaborating, respecting each other's views, and learning from one another is hard work. It also takes time, and we live in an impatient culture. We want to resolve our differences and resolve them now. We don't have the courage to allow differences to coexist in our programs and see what happens. Yet waiting and watching on the part of adults is what allows children in Reggio Emilia to accomplish what children in this country do not.

Alvin Toffler (1970, 414) quotes psychologist Herbert Gerjuoy in *Future Shock*: "Tomorrow's illiterate will not be the man who can't read; he will be the man who has not learned how to learn." One of the structural foundations of preschool in Reggio Emilia is the notion of the teacher as learner and researcher. Adults model the attitude that if an idea does not work, we'll try something else! In the United States, however, we tend to hold the idea that there is only one way to approach a job to achieve the desired outcome. Perhaps we should reflect on this attitude and ask ourselves "Why?" more frequently:

- Why must we be certain of an outcome before we begin a project?

- Why must children go down the slide feet first?

- Why not approach more ideas with, "I wonder what would happen if . . . ?"

- Why can't the children stand on a chair or table to make a structure higher?

- Why can't we pretend Unifix cubes are vegetables and stir them in a pot? Will it really hurt the math area? Does this really constitute a misuse of equipment?

- Why?

When I visit preschools around the country, I am often dismayed by the number of really good ideas from children that are rejected by adults as unsafe. I once worked in a school system that approached guidance and discipline with *safety* as one of the first and foremost concerns. The staff was asked to decide with children on a very few rules and consistently enforce them. In the early stages of discussion, the teachers came up with some very valid questions and perspectives:

- "We serve children ages three to six. Isn't it likely that what is safe for some is not safe for others?"

- "We have such a wide range of abilities. If we make rules based on the lowest limits of safety, will this remove the challenge for many others?"

- "I know children the same age whose understanding and self-control are very different. It makes me nervous to apply the same measure and consequences to all of them. Why can't the rules be child and teacher specific?"

That last one is my favorite! Somehow, we need to find a way to allow both children and teachers to fully utilize their strengths. We need to respect and accept children's and teachers' fears and misgivings in certain situations. I think we respect children's fears more than we respect each other's. We often slip into believing that our way is *the* way rather than accepting a variety of pedagogical approaches. By broadening our view, we can show children that diversity is beneficial for all of us.

Questions for Discussion

1. Do you think teachers in your program understand and agree with your center's policies and rules?

2. Does it bother you when a coworker has a completely different idea about how to accomplish a goal with the children? Why? What do you usually do about it?

3. Frequently, teachers will ban a behavior on a climbing structure because it would be unsafe for some children. Is this policy unfair to the children who have the physical skills to do it safely? Why or why not?

DISCIPLINE

21

Discipline

I have always loved the word *discipline*. It's a good word that has gotten a bad rap in the past few decades—especially from those of us who work in early childhood education. "I prefer to say *guidance*," a speaker said recently at a workshop. Teachers nodded their heads, smiling. Early childhood professionals speak passionately about children's behavior and comment that it seems to get worse every year. Even so, we don't want to say the word *discipline*, much less implement it in our work with children. I wonder if this hesitance is a contributing factor to the notion (and often the reality) that children are increasingly out of control both at home and at child care.

Discipline is an area where the pendulum of preferred practice seems to swings back and forth to extremes without ever settling in the middle. For years, behavior management seminars began by outlining the three primary modes of parenting and teaching:

1. Authoritarian: adults make all the calls.

2. Permissive: children make all the calls.

3. Democratic or authoritative: children have input and choice, but adults guide the process.

Adults who want to avoid the punitive harshness of authoritarian models often swing to the other extreme of permissiveness. Adults who want to avoid the overly lax nature of the permissive model often swing to authoritarian tactics. Both extremes are equally damaging to children.

I don't agree with the fear tactics or physical punishment that was common in the 1940s and 1950s, but I also know that young children look to the adults in their lives to help them control themselves until they have the self-regulation skills to manage it on their own. Children don't really want to kick and bite when they are enraged, but if no one teaches them what to do instead, they'll just communicate in the way that comes naturally to them.

Although I have empathy for the parent whose child kicks, hits, shouts, "I'm not ready!" and runs away at the end of the day, I also have sympathy for the child whose parents ignore this behavior and don't put a stop to it. It is quite possible to pick up most two- to six-year-old children and carry them kicking and screaming to the car. "I can see you don't like it, but it's time to go," the parent might say. I'll be the first to admit that confronting an angry teenager is scary, especially when the teenager's height and weight exceed yours by six inches and forty pounds, respectively. This is all the more reason to help children modify their antisocial behavior when they still weigh less than fifty pounds. Children need our help to learn what is inappropriate in these early years. They need our firm refusal to accept the kicking and biting, our understanding of their anger, and our ability to give them coping strategies. We need to show them what behaviors they can express instead.

When teaching courses on guiding children's behavior, I sometimes hear toddler teachers say, "I've got a real bully in my class!" This comment makes me shudder. To respond, I begin at the beginning. Babies are new to the planet, and they don't have the cognitive ability to plan an attack on another toddler:

- If a nineteen-month-old sees something interesting, she will walk right over someone's face to get to it.

- If a fourteen-month-old puts his finger in someone's eye, he is experimenting. It doesn't hurt his finger, so how could it hurt the other child's eye?

- We have low teacher–child ratios in infant/toddler classes for a reason. These little ones need maximum supervision and support.

- I've heard providers say, "If we could bite back, these babies would learn not to bite." No, they wouldn't. They would learn that might makes right!

We need to support infant/toddler exploration. We need to keep them safe. It isn't their job not to touch something hot, not to walk in front of a swing, and not to run into the street. It is our job to prevent all of these things.

I sometimes overhear parents discussing their disdain for the clothes their young daughters or sons wear. It is hard for me to imagine these five- and six-year-olds having the money, transportation, or even the height to reach the rack where clothes are purchased. We need to ask ourselves, Who is in charge here? Who bought the clothes these children are wearing?

The responsibility lies in the answers: *We* are in charge, and *we* probably bought the clothes. The adults in a culture are responsible for guiding and modeling behavior. Increasingly, we seem to be doing a less effective job. We tell little ones to use their words, not their hands, but we don't tell them which words to use or when to use them. Parents and providers can help children learn appropriate behavior in three ways:

1. acting the way we hope children will learn to act

2. patiently pointing out when children's behavior is not appropriate

3. telling them what they can do or say instead

Even when parents and teachers do a fair job at number two, many of us just never get to number one or number three. I frequently see teachers interrupting children, even though I also hear them reminding children not to interrupt. I have walked into buildings and heard a teacher shout at the top of her lungs, "I want quiet in here!" I have witnessed the ludicrous scene of a parent saying, "Don't you ever hit," while punctuating each word with a slap on the bum.

One of the best ways to actively teach children self-discipline is to be self-disciplined ourselves. Thousands of years ago, Plato (*Laws* 5.729c) gave us good advice, "The best way of training the young is to train yourself at the same time; not to admonish them, but to be seen always doing that of which you would admonish them." In other words, we need to behave the way we want the children in our care to behave. When we see a frustrated, angry baby pull another baby's hair or scratch someone, we get upset. And sometimes this behavior taps at ancient wounds in even the best of teachers. We become angry because an unsuspecting baby has a bloody scratch that we'll have to explain to parents. We forget to model a calm, caring response, which is how the babies in our care will learn to be calm and caring themselves.

It isn't easy to help young children grow. Sometimes we shout or slap due to fear, fatigue, or frustration. Few children are impaired for life because a parent or teacher acts out once in a while. It is the patterns of our behavior over time that make the difference. Accepting our occasional lapses humanizes both parents and teachers to children. In fact, these lapses provide us an opportunity to teach another important lesson: when we hurt each other in a moment of anger or fear, we can say we're sorry once it's over. When a child hears a grown-up say, "I'm sorry I yelled at you. I was afraid you were going to be hurt," the child learns that grown-ups make mistakes too and that telling people we're sorry makes everyone feel better!

Questions for Discussion

1. Should adults apologize to young children? Do you think apologizing makes parents and teachers appear stronger or weaker? Why do you think so?

2. Does your center agree about the cognitive ability of toddlers to understand hurting others? If there are differences of opinion, how do you deal with them?

3. As a group, generate four sentences describing firm, empathic, and nurturing responses to infant and toddler poking, hair pulling, and biting.

Do As I Say, or Do As I Do?

Many respected educators say that our relationship with children is the true curriculum; that is, who we are and how we are is the best measure of what we teach young children. A less academic expression of this idea comes from a bumper sticker I love, which reads "Children learn from example—the problem is they don't know a good one from a bad one." The concept that example *is* the curriculum is often absent from our discussions about teaching young children.

Today there is a renewed focus on being mindful and intentional when we plan activities for children. We spend huge sums of money on books, conferences, and courses to increase our proficiency at planning and implementing developmentally appropriate curricula. We've realized that, yes, play is the work of childhood, and children need the power to make choices for themselves, but mindless wandering shouldn't be mistaken for a rich and meaningful play experience. How do we know the difference?

In the history of early childhood education, we have gone through periods when adults did all of the planning and directing of children's daily activities. Teachers did not tune in to cues for an emergent curriculum or attend to the wonderful, spontaneous ideas that surface from children themselves. On the other side of the coin, we have gone through periods that trend too far in the opposite direction and have expected children to create meaningful activities for themselves without intentional planning and preparation on the part of teachers. Long before Katz or Kozol or Forman, John Dewey told us that teachers need to know what to teach young children. Planning essential experiences for children is important, but so is changing plans if children have other things on their minds.

Many of the ideas in this book come from other teachers I have worked with over the years. Some ideas came from Lilian Katz and George Forman. Others I read about in works by Margaret Mead and Rachel Carson. Most recently, I've drawn inspiration from Jonathan Kozol's book *Letters to a Young Teacher* (2007). I highly recommend it to all educators. Kozol wrote this book in response to the statistic than 50 percent of college-trained educators leave the field in less than five years. To Kozol and to me, this is a national tragedy.

As a thirty-year veteran in teacher education, I think part of the problem is that our curriculum for teachers on how to be a good teacher is not as strong as it should be. We often cover too much material too quickly and don't allow for any depth of understanding. Many teachers expect teaching to be easier and more predictable than it is. Teaching is hard work; don't let anyone tell you different.

When my youngest child was a senior in college, she and her three roommates were all education majors. All four worked their way through college in child care programs for children under age eight. On several occasions, I listened to the four of them talk about their experiences in programs for children. It was a humbling experience for me. Sometimes the mirror they held up to us was not flattering. Here are a few of the things I heard them say:

- "When I got really involved and engaged with the children, the head teacher said flatly, 'C'mon, take it easy. You're making us look bad.' It's like she wanted me not to care so much about doing a good job."

- "One of the teachers on the team went on break, and the lead teacher said to me, 'Watch out for her, she's a pompous jerk and not good with the kids.' I was so surprised by her lack of professionalism."

- "One of the teachers told me my head teacher doesn't know what she's doing. She claimed the head teacher was hired because she's a friend of the director."

All four of these young women heard teachers make demeaning comments about children, such as "She cries all the time just to get attention" or "He's way too aggressive" or "She's always trying to get her own way." These words were spoken right in front of the children, as if they were not there. It breaks my heart.

We don't spend nearly enough time teaching basic communication skills to educators. We need to work hard to communicate with children, their families, and—most of all—with each other. Miscommunication or limited communication between adults can lead to situations that adversely affect all parties involved. I think most of us have been in situations where poor or limited communication made a mess of our work life.

It was really hard for me to listen to my daughter and her roommates talk about the gossip, lack of empathy, and negativity at their early childhood workplaces. It reminded me of my first teaching position in 1968 when I walked into the faculty room and a veteran teacher gave me the lowdown on the families of the children in my class. Much of what she shared was gossip and wasn't relevant to teaching the eight-year-olds in my class. Before listening to my daughter and her friends, I was naive or optimistic enough to think we had grown beyond such discussions. Hearing that circumstances hadn't really changed was a bitter pill to swallow. Unfortunately, research confirms that 80 percent of early childhood educators avoid conflict and choose to gossip instead of confronting problems (Bruno and Copeland 1999).

Is gossip as alive and well in the early childhood education community as this research suggests? Or are early childhood authors and researchers making mountains out of mole hills? My experience leads me to believe that the authors have been easy on us. Children learn by observing us. When we worry about children being unkind to each other, we need to think about how we treat each other. This is easier with a small team of teachers. For those working in large programs, cliques develop more readily. Even so, the children are always watching and listening to us.

Jonathan Kozol (2007, 86) calls our behaviors "the secret curriculum." He says, "The secret curriculum in almost any class, in my belief, is not the message that is written in a lesson plan or a specific book but the message of implicit skepticism or, conversely, of passivity or acquiescence that is written in the teacher's eyes."

In my early years of teaching, educators were allowed to set out snacks and let children serve themselves when they were hungry. (Some programs across the country still do this, but sadly, not mine.) Peanut butter was a commonly used and well-loved snack at the time. So, when I saw a five-year-old boy licking the peanut-butter knife, I told him to stop because I was worried he'd hurt himself. His friend said, "Maybe she's worried about you, but I think she thinks you're a pig!" My words were the correct early childhood words, but my eyes apparently registered disgust. It taught me early on to strive for honesty, as tactfully as I can present it. Our authenticity does come through to children. If we find ourselves always having negative thoughts about our coworkers, the parents, or the children, we truly need to consider an attitude adjustment or possibly another line of work.

Bruno (2007) makes the point that listening to gossip is the same as gossiping. She calls on us to be proactive and to develop gossip-free zones in our workplaces. I have tried this in my professional life and had varying degrees of success. I believe we need to talk *to* each other, not *about* each other, but the research on this one is not in our favor. Sociologist Deborah Tannen (1994), whose books are well written and informative, says women tend to avoid confrontation and seek support from other women. I repeatedly observe this behavior in the workplace. Robin goes to her closet to get black construction paper. She is certain she has plenty. She opens the door and finds twenty sheets. Looking into the next classroom, she sees that Shelly has a brand-new bulletin board display: sparkly glitter spiderwebs on black construction paper. Robin is angry and justifiably so if the other teacher is supposed to use her own resources. But does Robin go to Shelly and say, "I'm feeling so frustrated. I planned an activity, and now I can't do it. I wish you had checked with me before using the black paper. What can we do to avoid this in the future?" No. As Tannen says, she more likely seeks support from other women. She trots down to Marian's room and says, "Can you believe her? Something should be done. I'm so sick of this! The stealing in this building is out of control." Marian is full of empathy. "You are so right. I heard she stole playdough from so-and-so last week!"

We fear direct confrontation. When we handle our frustration poorly, the entire staff is affected. Bruno (2007, 27) quotes Jamilah Jor'dan: "Gossip creates a work environment that is mean-spirited and impacts morale." I agree with her. She suggests we provide teachers with words to use to deflect participation in this negative dynamic. Here are some examples I share with my staff:

Teacher 1: Did you hear . . . blah blah blah?
Teacher 2: No . . . and I'd like to keep it that way!

Teacher 1: She is so disorganized!
Teacher 2: She does seem to have a lot on her mind.

Teacher 1: I can't believe she would think that's okay!
Teacher 2: We are certainly a diverse group!

Teacher 1: How could they think that?
Teacher 2: Well, you know what they say—if everyone thinks the same thing, no one is really thinking!

Teacher 1: Are you okay?
Teacher 2: Well, I was until I walked into the office and got another chore dumped on my plate!
Teacher 1: I hear you! So much work, so little time.

Teacher 1: Who submitted that new application form? I thought I recognized the name—boy are they an involved family!
Teacher 2: I'm trying to remember—we may have had a sibling.

Teacher 1: I heard the training last week was really pointless. Did you go?
Teacher 2: Yes, and there were some good points made! It's disappointing when a workshop doesn't meet your needs, but I learned some tips. I'm glad I went.

Teacher 1: She's always waltzing in here a half hour late. If I tried that, I'd be getting my pink slip!

Teacher 2: She could have a standing medical appointment or something. We don't know, and we're not her supervisor.

Teacher 1: If you don't want to spend time with kids, why have them? I get frustrated when parents leave their children with us from 6:30 in the morning until 5:30 at night.

Teacher 2: I heard at a conference last year that early childhood programs can be a link to safe childhoods, giving parents needed respite. Some parents struggle.

Bruno (2007, 32) concludes the article by asking the question, "Does venting help or hurt?" She tells us, "Some people need to vent or express their upset feelings before they can calm down to problem solve." But she also says, "Venting per se not only does not solve the problem, but can also be gossiping."

In *Anger: The Misunderstood Emotion*, Carol Tavris (1989) analyzes the conventional wisdom that those who rant and rave are healthier than those who don't, reflecting on the "I don't get ulcers; I give them" idea. Her research proves that ranting and raving only makes people angrier than they already are. And in the workplace, anger is as contagious as strep throat! Children suffer when they observe our negative body language as we whisper stories about our colleagues. Even when we tell ourselves that the children are napping, we know that they are watching—always. Our body language speaks volumes. If relationships and example are the curriculum, we need to bring positive attitudes to work with us. Venting should be done at home to partners or friends—where it won't jeopardize the staff's or children's morale.

As early childhood educators, we often tell each other that we can help children know *what not to do* by telling them *what to do* instead. In that spirit, I'd like to share the guidance of Professor Lilian Katz, who published a small volume called *Talks with Teachers* in 1977. I carried a page from *Talks with Teachers* with me for decades and made it a part of every course I ever taught. Just as I urge you to read Kozol's *Letters to a Young Teacher*, I urge you to consider this thirty-year-old excerpt about meeting the needs of young children:

CHILDREN'S NEEDS FOR DEVELOPMENT

The young child has to have a deep sense of safety.

Every child has to have adequate, not excessive, self-esteem.

Every child has to feel or experience life as worth living, reasonably satisfying, interesting, and authentic.

Young children need adults or older children to help them make sense of their own experience.

Young children have to have adults who accept the authority that is theirs by virtue of their greater experience, knowledge, and wisdom.

Young children need optimum associations with adults and older children who exemplify the personal qualities we want them to acquire.

Children need relationships or experiences with adults who are willing to take a stand on what is worth doing, worth having, worth knowing, and worth caring about.

Adapted with permission from Katz (1977).

The wisdom in Katz's words continue to be a timely reminder. We need to be an inspiration to children—and to the youngest generation of teachers who care for them. We need to champion the positive, caring attributes we all need to survive on our small planet. The pressure of No Child Left Behind and intense accountability for meeting learning objectives will rob children of enthusiastic teachers. We should mourn the sense of wonder that teachers once brought to the workplace. Children need teachers who laugh and play and value imagination and creativity. Children need teachers who love what they do and show it in all they do. We have a battle ahead of us—not just about the tone and style of a child's education—but also about the purpose of that education and how teachers can deliver it. What should our curriculum be?

For centuries we have known that if we want children to be reared with certain principles, we must carry out those principles in practice ourselves. We need to behave the way we want children to, period. It isn't easy, but that is our challenge. We need to model for and inspire the next generation. The children and young teachers are watching and learning from all that we do. We are the curriculum!

Questions for Discussion

1. Do you think Kozol is correct when he says that teacher behavior is a secret curriculum?

2. Do early childhood educators engage in gossip at work? Why do you think they do it? Why do you think some refrain from participating?

3. What is the most significant element missing in most teacher education programs?

Problem Behavior: Is It Escalating?

I live in a fairly small state. Two years ago, an hour away from where I live, teenagers killed a young woman and brutally attacked her daughter. From all reports, it was a random act of violence. A resident of the tiny community who has teenagers herself said the boys involved were on Facebook within hours of the crime, discussing what a fun time it was. When we hear such stories (and we do hear about them in today's 24/7 news world), we wonder, how can this happen? What would make young boys go to a randomly selected home, kill a woman, and attack her young daughter, leaving her perhaps to bleed to death? What kind of conscience would allow these boys to joke about it the same evening? These are hard questions. There are no easy answers.

During the past decade, possibly two, early childhood educators have felt increasing discomfort about how to interact with children when their behavior is hurtful, dangerous, or unacceptable in some way. Teachers are perplexed, unsure of themselves, and even afraid. In a typical swinging pendulum fashion, the goal of eliminating harsh and hurtful responses to negative behaviors soon eroded into a lack of direction, confusion, or an apologetic acceptance of any behavior as appropriate.

This trend has affected both teaching and parenting to an extent that is frightening to observe. Here are some scenarios that may be familiar to you:

Grandma picks up five-year-old Emily from preschool. Emily wants to go out to lunch. Grandma says they don't have time today. Emily starts screaming, kicking, and shouting, "It's not fair!" Grandma, embarrassed, says, "Emily, I'm sorry to disappoint you, but we have to go home today." With extreme physical energy, Grandma pulls Emily, kicking and screaming, to the car.

• • • • •

Kim is a newly graduated preschool teacher. Her college course work prepared her to make great prop boxes, extend stories, engage children with puppets and playdough, and introduce reading through writing. Her courses helped her to know that partnering with families is important, as is cultural diversity. It did not, however, adequately prepare her for five-year-olds who use profanity, children who hit each other with hardwood blocks, or parents who insist that curiosity led kindergartners to flush puppets down the toilet. Kim wants to adequately partner with parents but is paralyzed by the children's behavior and the parental stance on curiosity.

• • • • •

Heather loved her early childhood education classes in college, and she had a great experience as a student-teacher in kindergarten and second-grade classrooms. Now, as a first-grade teacher, she knows that teaching reading is critical, but she feels unsure of herself. Her colleagues expect her to know what to do. After all, she has a bachelor's degree in education. She doesn't know how well her first graders are doing. One day, Heather put her hands on Tina's face and said, "I need you to look at me when I'm talking to you." Tina told her mother that Heather hit her in the face. The mother called the principal. Heather doesn't want to be a part of the statistic that 50 percent of teachers leave the field in five years (National Education Association 2011), but after the incident with Tina, Heather wonders if she'll make it.

• • • • •

Dawn was laid off from her prekindergarten position in the inner city when her state put a freeze on early childhood education support for low-income families. After three months of searching, she finds a toddler position in a nearby affluent suburb. The transition in both age range and economic conditions is not easy for Dawn. The biggest challenge, however, is what to do with the eight two-year-olds:

- Two of them are very oral and put anything, including their peers' fingers, in their mouths.

- One of the families insists that their twenty-two-month-old is ready to use the toilet. Dawn has observed no signs of readiness.

- The director is very clear that the program is NAEYC accredited and that she has no tolerance for negativity. Saying "No" is forbidden in the staff handbook.

• • • • •

I wonder if there is a connection between adults' minimal expectations of children's behavior and adolescents who think taking someone's life is a joke. Though the example of the teenagers is extreme, it is also real. If we do not tell children that hurting others is wrong, how will they know?

About twenty years ago, journalist Bill Moyers (1988) interviewed pediatrician T. Berry Brazelton about the state of family life in the United States. He asked Brazelton what would happen in a country where citizens chose not to invest in the needs of the next generation. Usually an optimist, Brazelton raised his hands in a rather hopeless gesture and responded simply, "Look around you."

Early childhood educators study Erik Erikson's stages of development. We learn that acquiring a sense of trust is the first task of an infant. Developing a strong independent sense of self comes next. Learning to take initiative follows. Throughout these stages, the presence of caring and guiding adults is critical. Children depend on us to help them control themselves until they can regulate their own behavior, and sometimes they need support even after they have developed these skills. If adults turn the other way when children hurt each other or disrupt the learning space of others, everyone loses. Children can't learn if we don't help them. They will not develop empathy and kindness without our modeling and direct teaching. When we ignore negative behavior continually, children begin to believe it is okay to hurt themselves and others. They need our help. Too many of us have not provided that help.

Teachers know that it takes a long time to develop social skills. We know that children need help learning how to enter a group and how to resolve differences. Quite sadly, teachers often fall into thinking that children will grow into these behaviors on their own. This is not true. We need to calmly but firmly say, "I can't let you hit. Hitting hurts. Tell her it's yours." We need to accept that we will have to repeat this message over and over again in the context of daily preschool conflict. In a few years, and with constant enforcement, these guidelines will become part of how children think.

It's funny how we usually don't hear teachers use impatient voices or say, "How many times do I have to tell you?" when the task is remembering which character is the letter *B* and which is *D*. When children are upset and need our help to use words and not fists, however, we act like the lack of skill is intentional. This attitude doesn't help children very much. We need to remember that children are learning how to behave and that it takes time. Appropriate behavior is not like height. It will not develop without adult direction.

Thinking of discipline as a form of teaching is essential to building skills as an early childhood educator. We are all quick to bring up Gardner's theory of multiple intelligences when planning our curriculum. We remind parents and children that none of us are good at everything; some of us are good at math, others at music. That empathetic understanding is often missing when we deal with the child who struggles with remembering social rules or situations. For some reason, we think once is enough when we say, "I can't let you hit." Even the language we use to describe behavioral learning is different from other areas of the curriculum. I've never heard a teacher say, "She has a real attitude problem about shapes, numbers, and color." When it comes to listening and keeping hands to oneself, however, we expect children to learn quickly and permanently, which is something they are not yet capable of.

Of course, a child who can't remember which shape is a square and which is a rectangle is less distracting to classroom life than a child who can't remember whether to ask for help or to bite someone.

But our job is to support each child in everything that child is learning. For children, all learning takes time and practice. We also need to remember that our tone of voice, body language, and facial expressions impact our messages to children. We have to train ourselves to use a firm and serious voice and expression when telling children they need to stop a behavior. If a sugary sweet voice and smile accompany the words "I can't let you hit," children will not get the message.

Young teachers are told to always phrase things in the positive, but there are times when "No!" "Stop!" and "Don't even think about it!" are appropriate responses to children's behaviors. A rock poised in an angry little hand or teeth moving in to bite another child are examples of when these responses are sensible. Firm redirection is in the best interest of the child. You can explain your response in a calm manner after the child stops the action. Remember, she is learning.

Questions for Discussion

1. Have you ever heard a colleague respond to a child's behavior in a way that seemed too harsh? What did you do? Were you pleased with the result? Why or why not?

2. Is it appropriate for teachers to express anger in front of very young children? Why or why not?

3. Do most of the parents of children in your care respond confidently to their children's positive and negative behaviors? How do you know?

An Impulse for Impulse Control

W hen I heard sound bites on ABC News about preschool expulsion rates, I initially rolled my eyes and thought, what next? When the news piece referenced the Zigler Center in Child Development and Social Policy at Yale University, however, I chose not to dismiss the piece as "media propaganda" after all; I knew the credibility of Yale's research. Walter Gilliam, director of the Zigler Center at the time, said that he stumbled upon the preschool expulsion data when he was analyzing preschool policies in publicly funded programs. He found expulsion rates in preschool to be three times higher than in older grades. In an attempt to explain the findings, Gilliam cited anecdotal reports from teachers who believed behavioral problems in children had been increasing; scientific data to support the claims had not been conducted. Gilliam (quoted in James 2008) stressed that "expulsions set children up for educational failure." He gave recommendations for prevention: "better teacher training, smaller classes, and increased support from psychologists and social workers." A statement from NAEYC was included in the news report; the organization said simply, "We agree with the findings."

The number of *former* preschool teachers referenced in the news piece bothered me. It reminded me of discussions I once had with a previous supervisor. This particular program had an established policy to "serve every child." I argued with my supervisor about several children whose behavior was so out of control that it scared the other children. I mentioned that three good teachers had left the center and the early childhood field because of their frustrating and failed attempts to make it work with these children. What is a program to do? Digging deeper and reflecting on Gilliam's recommendations, I realized that I found sociology and psychology majors a better match for managing children than the early childhood educators our state credentialing system required.

Many creative young women and men with degrees in early childhood education take teaching positions armed with what they consider to be tools of the trade. Many of these young teachers have seen the Hundred Languages of Children exhibit. They know about Caldecott Medal–winning books and sensory experiences that will delight typical preschoolers. Still, some of these teachers quit before they've spent three months in the classroom. They know what to do with clay and fingerpaint, but they have no idea how to face four-year-olds who are shouting the *F*-word, throwing blocks and chairs across the room, or biting teachers from behind. They have no idea how to redirect the behavior while comforting children who are frightened by it. These teachers are often reduced to tears and feelings of resignation in a job they've always wanted to do. Child guidance, discipline, and guiding behavior have always been high on the list of desired workshops for early childhood educators. It seems the need for these workshops and the behaviors they address are both on the rise.

According to many preschool teachers, parents regularly say to them, "I have no idea what to do with my child!" A similar, but not often addressed, sentiment is prevalent among early childhood educators. Teachers were once told to phrase everything in the positive; never say "No" to young children. They are now being told to emphasize self-control and self-regulation. Adults don't know what to do, and somewhere deep down, children know it.

Years ago when I taught courses on guiding children's behavior, the three models of parenting and teaching—authoritarian, permissive, and democratic (see essay 21)—were the foundation on which most adults built their approach to teaching appropriate behaviors. Because I grew up when the authoritarian approach was the norm, I still find it challenging to describe it in a positive light. Even so, as a child I always understood that the grown-ups were in charge and knew what to do. Once, after a particularly intense argument with my fourteen-year-old son, I overheard him comment to his sixteen-year-old brother, "Yeah, man, I had her scared. I could tell by the look on her face." His observation upset me far more than the conflict itself, because I knew it was true and I knew it wasn't good for him or for me. In spite of my many mistakes and indecisions, however, my children all hold jobs, seem fairly typical, and still speak to me on a regular basis.

When parents say, "I just don't know what to do!" or worse; when we recommend outside supports to families whose six-year-olds growl, scratch, bite, and kick when they don't get what they want immediately; when the parental response is, "Well, he's just a small child and he's feeling frustrated," I worry for all of us. I believe we were on the right track years ago when we started recommending the democratic (or authoritative) approach as a good middle ground between harsh authoritarianism and squishy, dangerous permissiveness. I believe that the pendulum has swung way too far to the side of permissiveness.

Some people think the increase in children's social aggression is a reflection on parents. I agree with this to some extent, but I also believe it is a cultural fallacy to blame parents and look the other way. If I hear one more senior citizen protest rising taxes for the sake of improving town schools, I may have to move abroad. Children are the responsibility of all of us. We need to speak to children and adolescents on our streets and communities whether we are parents or not. We need to support schools in our communities whether we are parents or not. We need to vote at work and at the polls for policies that support young families—whether we have one or not.

Trite as it may seem, the sayings "It takes a village to raise a child" and "The children are our future" are true. It's up to all of us to make sure we protect and nurture growing children. It's up to all of us to know what to do; if we don't, they'll know by the look on our faces. It's simple: they need us, and we need them. That's the future.

Questions for Discussion

1. As a staff, discuss the three models of parenting and teaching. In what ways do you agree about them? In what ways do you disagree?

2. What factors contribute to the cultural tendency in this country to take extreme positions on serious issues rather than find a balance?

3. Do staff members in your program agree about how to handle discipline issues? If not, how do you manage the differences?

Practice Makes Perfect

It was the last week of kindergarten. The "stepping-up" ceremony, as it has come to be known since the word *graduation* became passé, was about to begin. The children were excited. They had songs to sing and two- or four-line poems to recite for grandparents, aunties, siblings, and parents, who were all gathered at our little school for the last time. Family members' cameras and video recorders were at the ready to preserve the moment forever. Strawberries and lemonade were prepared for the children and families to enjoy after the ceremony. The children met their teachers as families and friends took seats. Unfamiliar to each other in bow ties, vests, fancy dresses, and curls, the children smiled shyly or grinned broadly as they waited for their moment to be front and center.

The excitement and high expectations of this kind of moment are represented frequently in old reruns of *Little House on the Prairie* or *Anne of Green Gables*. These moments, however, have almost disappeared from the early childhood landscape in the past twenty years. We don't want children to feel on the spot. We don't want them to work hard at recitation or, even worse, rely on the prompting of their friends to get through this experience. But all of these things will prepare children for real life.

In her book *The Self-Esteem Trap: Raising Confident and Compassionate Kids in an Age of Self-Importance*, Polly Young-Eisendrath discusses parents who channel unresolved anxieties into their child rearing. These parents and teachers often misunderstand what fosters self-esteem and self-confidence. Self-esteem and self-confidence,

Young-Eisendrath (2008, 48) writes, "do not come from liking your-self or being praised just for being. Self-esteem and self-confidence are by-products of doing things well, developing an attitude of self-respect through recognizing your actual strengths and weaknesses, knowing how to be ordinary, and learning the rules and benefits of interdependence, including how to fit into a hierarchy as a beginner and how to learn from elders. Unknowingly, the Boomers [Baby Boomers] designed child-rearing practices that left their children with the symptoms of being special, instead of a solid foundation for self-confidence and good self-esteem."

At our stepping-up ceremony, I observed two perfect examples of how too much praise, or praise lacking authenticity, nurtures a lack of self-confidence rather than the opposite. Sparkling performances (all two minutes of them) were rendered by the class clown, the quiet little one whose parents were thrilled because he now jokes with friends occasionally, and most of our well-loved motley crew. The most articulate and advanced kindergartners, however, froze, cried, and refused the help of peers ready to jump in—the interdependence Young-Eisendrath speaks of. Months before, in response to a question about her swimming lessons, one of these children said to me, "My mother wants me to be good at everything." She seemed sad and overburdened when she spoke. Being good at everything is a great deal of pressure for a five-year-old.

I am grateful that I raised my children before the No Child Left Behind legislation and before "motherhood in the age of anxiety" (Warner 2006). I raised my children to take time to smell the roses, watch a sunset, and help friends, perhaps because I was an educator and had been influenced by David Elkind's book *The Hurried Child: Growing Up Too Fast Too Soon*. Admittedly, the 1970s and 1980s offered safer neighborhoods where, perhaps, more neighbors knew each other. More importantly, though, it was a time when professionals urged parents to leave kids alone for at least some part of the day. Elkind (1981, 31) writes, "Generally, it is parent need, not a child's authentic wish, that pushes children into team sports at an early age. School-age children need the opportunity to play their own games, make up their own rules, abide by their own timetable. Adult intervention interferes with the crucial learning that takes place when children arrange their own games."

Still, the majority of five-year-olds in my school are enrolled in adult-organized baseball, soccer, gymnastics, dance, Tae Kwon Do, or all of the above. In the Northeast, the winner of the preschool-pressure prize in sports goes to hockey. Whole families get up at three o'clock in the morning and spend weekends in neighboring states (wherever ice time is available) so a five-year-old has a better chance for acceptance at Harvard, Dartmouth, or Yale on a hockey scholarship.

I have fond memories of my children learning to ice-skate; they pushed a small chair across the side yard, which their dad flooded every winter for this purpose. Yet, as a college freshman, one son came home insisting that we hadn't nurtured excellence. He was certain that eighteen was way too late in life to get good at anything!

Child care providers know that young children today do not get enough sleep at night. Some of the children are exhausted on a continual basis. Pediatricians will recommend at least ten hours for most young children, but many are fortunate to get even seven. In addition, family life is often so busy that it allows no time for chores, family meals, or neighborhood play, which are all necessary for learning that cooperation, effort, and getting along with others are equally as important as being "good" at something.

During the last week of school, I read a story to the children about a little boy who struggles to control his angry feelings. In the story, the mother encourages the boy in his small successes. She tells her child that it usually takes a great deal of practice to get good at something. I asked the children if they knew what *practice* meant. I was discouraged to hear a chorus of answers singing out, "baseball," "soccer," and "hockey." But, then, one child raised his hand and said slowly, "No. Practice is when you can't do something. You want to do it. You see other people who can do it, but you don't give up. You keep trying and trying, and finally you can do it too. That's practice!"

Educators fear that kindergartners like this one will become even rarer if we continue to push children to participate in and develop only those skills for which they demonstrate a strong ability. We connect effort and practice as an approach to competence too rarely.

Overemphasis on being special, learning for fun, and everyone being excellent has robbed many of our children of the gifts of effort, persistence, and accepting average as an okay standard.

In the conclusion to his outstanding volume *Huck's Raft: A History of American Childhood*, Steven Mintz talks about nostalgia for simpler childhoods. He references Huck Finn's abusive father, the town drunk who beat him for going to school. "Who would envy Huck's battered childhood?" Mintz (2004, 384) asks. "Yet he enjoyed something too many children are denied and which adults can provide: opportunities to undertake odysseys of self-discovery outside the goal-driven, over-structured realities of contemporary childhood."

Questions for Discussion

1. Does your program emphasize learning for fun over teaching children that learning new skills takes hard work and practice?

2. How much extracurricular activity do you think is too much for four- and five-year-olds? Do all of the staff members in your program agree with you?

3. Within the parameters of your day and curriculum, what can you do to offer children more opportunities to work out their own difficulties at play and free-choice time?

CARING COMMUNITIES

26

Child Care Communities for Families

We keep a variety of brochures for families in the front hall of our child care center. The brochures include tips on temper tantrums, dying grandparents, sibling relationships, terminal illnesses, new babies, dealing with bullies, divorce, sharing, and making friends, as well as other topics. On the family bulletin board, we keep information that helps children's families see the many ways our play stations help children learn. We also display a small but powerful poster that states, "To know how child care feels to parents, you need to stand in their shoes."

Several copies of Anne Stonehouse's book *How Does It Feel? Child Care from a Parent's Perspective* (1995) are available in our staff library. We work hard to make families feel welcome. We assure them that, to us, *family* means all the important people in a child's daily life. For children whose parents don't live in the same home, we put double notices—one for each parent—in their cubbies. At graduation, we create two diplomas for these children so both parents have a memory of the special day. We refuse to participate in discussions that malign other family members. We don't take sides.

Even further, we send notices to families reminding them how important grandparents are and how Dad's girlfriend or boyfriend and Mom's boyfriend or girlfriend are significant parts of the child's world. We talk openly about how hard it is for families to cope with the pain of divorce without maligning their former partner. As adults, however, it is our job to be civil and courteous and to assure children that we all have their best interests at heart, even if we have to fake it now and then.

In another corner of our entranceway, we house a collection of teacher-made books for the children to look at. They contain photos, anecdotes, observations, children's drawings, and interesting things that the children say. There are photos of children asleep at naptime— something parents often worry about. The observations are formal and informal, funny and serious. One teacher also arranged a family-portrait area in the housekeeping cottage where each child has a family photo or two framed on the wall.

All of these supports are easy to create and, according to our families, make a huge difference in how comfortable they feel when they leave their child for the day. In spite of these carefully planned strategies to connect with parents, problems still arise. Children lose hats or mittens that families can't afford to replace. Families get busy, forget to read memos, and then blame us when they have to scramble for care on a teacher planning day, even though a notice had been posted for three weeks. Educators and parents bicker, if you will, like most families.

It is exciting to ponder the possibilities for child care as the new millennium's extended family. We can exchange hand-me-downs. We can share care when the center is closed. We can share meals and talk honestly about how scared we get when we're not sure which path to take on discipline or development issues. We can plan playdates, commiserate, laugh at our own missteps, and share ideas that have worked for us.

Sometimes early childhood professionals who are not parents feel we go too far. Sometimes new teachers think we don't hold parents accountable enough. Sometimes they are right, but most young families are struggling just to get by. Their children are bombarded by media and other influences that families didn't have to think about forty years ago. Parents are logging more hours in the workplace. Parents' expectations for their jobs as parents exceed those of previous generations (Warner 2006). Helping young staff members understand the many challenges of the modern family is a critical responsibility for program directors. Many young educators are just beginning their careers and haven't pondered the many pressures on families today. Helping them to see how an us-versus-them attitude hurts everyone—especially the children, whom we all want to support—is crucial.

Teachers judging parents and parents judging teachers are old problems and touchy issues in our field. Long ago, before I was a parent, I was sure *my* children would never take missteps. Actually becoming a parent was such a humbling experience. Before I had children, I found it so easy to talk about parenting well. After I had children, I realized that parenting well was more difficult to achieve than I imagined. New teachers often feel that parents judge them because they are not parents, which is probably true to some extent. It is easier to hold strong, passionate beliefs about parenting issues when you are not a parent. Parents also feel judged by teachers. Plus, they feel judged by politicians, law enforcement agencies, media, and everyone else who often blames parenting as the root cause to most childhood problems.

Parenting in 2011, it seems to me, is harder than parenting was in 1981. We need to reach out to families we serve, understand their challenges, and offer supports in every way we can. This is even more important because the United States is not known for its family-friendly policies in workplaces or communities. Even worse, we live in a country where policies regarding family life are almost nonexistent:

- Commercial profit is a higher priority than family life, and little regard is given to harmful advertising that is directed at children.

- Many workplaces don't have paid-time-off policies for parents whose children are ill.

- The quality of medical care and education available to children is primarily based on socioeconomic status.

- We worship the rights of the individual, refusing to acknowledge the impact of community and culture (wealth or poverty) on the well-being of our children.

- We have strong data from the Perry Preschool Project (Schweinhart et al. 2005) on the positive effects of prevention but continue to put money into prisons rather than quality child care. We spend money to house individuals whose lives could have been different with early intervention and support.

We live in a country where free speech is honored, so I can say these things without fear of retribution. The fact remains: we are a country that is not making decisions based on the best interests of the next generation.

For those of you enthusiastically entering our profession and wanting to "save the children," here are a few free tips: Be gentle, develop compassion, and put yourself in a parent's shoes. Make your mantra "All parents want what is best for their children." Do what you can to support them. By doing so, you are laying the foundation for the future.

Questions for Discussion

1. Have you ever heard discussions or felt staff tension regarding the idea that teachers who are parents have a better understanding of parent issues than teachers who are not? If so, how did you feel? Has your program ever had a formal discussion about this tender topic? Why or why not?

2. Are there ways your program could better support families in their parenting role? Generate a list.

3. Have you ever heard an early childhood educator say, "If they didn't want to do a good job of parenting, why did they have kids?" What was the context? How did you respond?

27

The Permanence of Parents as Partners

The early childhood field does a wonderful job of talking about parent participation, parent-provider relationships, and parents as children's first teachers. In his book *Places for Childhood: Making Quality Happen in the Real World*, for example, Jim Greenman (1998) reminds us that places for childhood need to include parents. It seems we still have a hard time putting this theory into practice.

The United States has always been great at blaming the victim. I don't want to go on record as characterizing parents as victims, but it seems to me that parents are victimized by our culture in many ways that affect our parenting skills and behaviors. Public policy, nightly news, and screen and print media do more to blame parents than to support them.

In the 1970s, articles in *Young Children* and *Childhood Education* cautioned us against holding an us-versus-them mentality toward parents. We need to be partners. Mutual respect is key, our professional journals told us. In the 1980s, providers were urged to use terms like *the grown-up at your house* rather than *mom* or *dad* to respond to rising divorce rates. Despite high-quality advice to teachers about accepting all families, I'll bet I'm not the only educator who has heard colleagues say with pity, "It is a broken family, you know!" By the 1990s we'd all become accustomed to asking for all individuals' last names on intake forms, because "the important grown-ups in a child's life" (using our term from the 1980s) usually included a mix of grandparents, stepparents, uncles, and significant others. I'd like to remind us all that fifty years ago these connections were referred to as *extended family*.

As time marches on, we still regularly struggle to collaborate with the multitude of adults in children's lives. A family in which one or two adults act as the sole providers of care constitutes a shrinking percentage of all families in this country. Our language, policies, and children's books, however, still cling to a narrow vision of family as Mom and Dad, Dick and Jane, Spot and Puff.

Just last week, a mom brought in a costume for a play that was being held at the end of the week. As she left, the mom said, "I hope it will still be here when he needs it." That night the dad, who had been told by his ex-wife to leave the costume in the cubby, had to work late. He called his dad, the child's grandfather, who was stuck in traffic. The grandfather then called his other son, the child's uncle. (All of these adults were on our pickup list for the child.) The uncle picked up his nephew that evening and conscientiously emptied his cubby of all contents. The day of the play came, and the costume was in the corner of the uncle's home, far from the center. While the other children were full of excitement and sharing enthusiastic exchanges about the play, our young friend, usually bouncy and boisterous, sat quietly with a long face. We all felt bad, but we quickly realized we simply needed to be resourceful. As in most early childhood centers, we were equipped to do so. Teachers found costumes in dramatic-play areas and gathered fabric and accessories from art shelves and storage boxes. In fifteen minutes, the child was appropriately outfitted and grinning. Kids are interesting. Sometimes we waste so much energy pointing fingers, we forget that kids don't care *who* put the pieces in place, they just care that the pieces are in place and that no one looks down at them or their families. We all pulled together for this kid, whose huge family cared passionately about him. We cared passionately about him too.

I have supervised programs where this situation would have been handled differently. Below is a sample of what might have been said:

- "Parents need to take responsibility for their kids."

- "Didn't they know he would be upset?"

- "Do we have to do everything?"

- "If you're not going to be there for your kid, why have one?"

Here is what would have been done about the child's missing costume: *nothing*.

The world is increasingly complex. Child care is not neat and tidy. Neither is parenting. For those who really care about making a difference for the next generation, I suggest reading family historian Stephanie Coontz's works *The Way We Never Were* (1992) and *The Way We Really Are* (1997). Both books expose both liberal and conservative myths about family life in days gone by. We need to take responsibility for forming new ideas about how families look, and we need to make known what we expect from the public and the media in how we perceive and portray families and diversity. Finish your study of families with *(Mis)Understanding Families: Learning from Real Families in Our Schools* (Marsh and Turner-Vorbeck 2010). This book will give us all, I hope, some perspective on partnering with all families.

Times have changed. They always do. Families look different. They always have. Grown-ups need to be in charge. It's our responsibility and always has been. The future, we like to say, is the children. The responsibility for how that looks is ours. It is our responsibility as early childhood educators to have books, DVDs, and policies in place that say, "We are a community. We are a family. Friends are families who choose each other. There are many different ways for families to look, and at our program, all are welcome!"

Questions for Discussion

1. If you hear a new teacher in your program say that a child comes from a "broken home," how would you respond? Would other teachers in your program agree with your response?

2. In your program, have you ever had parents who seemed so disengaged from their children that you wondered why they even had them? If so, what did you do about it? With whom did you discuss the problem?

3. If a family in your program says to you that a lesbian couple is not really a family and should not be presented as such to children, how would you respond?

Politically Correct or Not?

At a discussion group, child care directors talked about open-ended activities for children during outdoor play. Their toddler teachers seemed pretty sure about boundaries and safety, but teachers from multiage classes of four-, five-, and six-year-olds, were not as comfortable. Discussion focused on individual differences and competencies. One young woman hesitated to let older children climb high on a climbing structure, even though they were capable, because she felt bad for the children who were not yet able. Another woman wondered if it was appropriate to let children climb in the small trees that framed their playground. Another person struggled with whether she should have let creativity run wild when children picked up quilts after snacktime and draped them over chairs to make forts. "It seemed such a 'kids and summer' thing to do," she said. "But the quilts weren't see-through, so I worried about licensing and visibility." Another person joined the conversation, "Remember making tepees with blankets when you were a child? . . . Wait! Are we supposed to say *tepee*?" This comment moved the conversation in a whole different direction.

"Ugh. Politically correct," chimed in one of the directors, who then recounted a story of being corrected by her supervisor for referring to an Asian family in her care as *Oriental*. "I feel like I can't keep up with the pace of things anymore!" she concluded, sounding very discouraged. The director was embarrassed because she cared deeply about respecting all of her families and didn't know she had made a misstep. When she was younger, most people from Asian countries were called *Oriental*. She felt awkward to have made the error, and she didn't want her colleagues to think she didn't respect all of her families. She just didn't know the term was offensive.

After the meeting, I thought long and hard about change and how rapid it has been in the past quarter of a century. I was recently struck by the fact that the names of chain restaurants have gotten more concise in the past decade. Think about it. No one says International House of Pancakes anymore. We meet for breakfast at IHOP. Burger King is BK. Kentucky Fried Chicken is now KFC. Most of us don't want to admit that we occasionally fall back on fast-food meals when we're in a pinch, but we all know and are more comfortable admitting that the families we serve do so regularly.

I'm usually the first one in a group to speak enthusiastically about leaders who inspire others to participate in civil rights, gay rights, or women's rights to make our country better for all of us. I also know that change takes time, and we need to give each other the benefit of the doubt. I often feel like the young woman in the director's group who said, "I just can't keep up!" Correcting others in a public place is not an effective way to make change. We stress the importance of being nonjudgmental to the families we serve but don't offer the same courtesy to each other.

Jumping on bandwagons is always tempting, but change with a lot of potential can fail if a transition is made too quickly without consideration to process and reflection. I remember, for example, the hasty switch to open education in this country. Open, or informal, education is a model that works very well for many children. Sadly, many school districts arbitrarily termed their primary schools "open" by tearing down classroom walls and arranging teachers in teams without the introduction, education, or ongoing support necessary to make any change successful. Parents were angry, teachers were frustrated, and children were not successful. Many of us who support open education as a successful alternative were disappointed that a good model, poorly implemented, was declared a foolish failure.

As I listen to providers around the country, I sometimes think we have made the same mistake regarding multicultural education. At the same gathering where the young woman apologized for using the word *tepee*, another woman complained that she was encouraged to celebrate the Chinese New Year, Cinco de Mayo, and Kwanzaa at her program, but she was not allowed to celebrate Christmas, which was the only celebration regularly exercised by the four -and five-year-olds in her small, rural New Hampshire community. The topic of holidays can draw out passionate and diverse points of view. I know from talking to hundreds of child care professionals that this is one of the biggest pendulum issues in our field. Like the provider wondering why she could only introduce children to holidays they didn't celebrate at home, many teachers are perplexed and even resentful about their program's position on celebrations with children.

If we look at developmentally appropriate practices (DAP) and the idea that we should teach to what is near and immediate in children's lives, then it makes no sense to introduce children in rural New Hampshire or Vermont to Cinco de Mayo while refusing to let them sing "Jingle Bells" in December. Many years ago, before the DAP book was published by NAEYC, and we were all just trying to figure out what would best support the lives of children, I relied heavily on publications from the Bank Street College of Education to inform my practice. In a wonderful volume for parents, the authors describe holidays as the "dependable milestones that mark off the seasons and the years in each child's life" (Bank Street College of Education 1981, 236). This definition sounds so benign today. We have become accustomed to viewing any celebration of traditional holidays as an affront to children's right to their own unique values. The Bank Street College publication suggests that even though we often forget the values we hold dear, celebrating holidays offers us a chance to reaffirm our values with the children in our lives.

When we work in programs that provide care and support to families from diverse backgrounds, we need to think of introducing any celebration as one that *some* of us celebrate *in this particular way*. To decide to do nothing or to insist on introducing children in New Mexico to Christmas as celebrated in New England is to miss the point of helping children understand the world in which we live.

Don't throw the baby out with the bathwater! If DAP urges us to build on experiences familiar to the young children in our care, then jumping to international celebrations without exploring the children's own holidays seems a poor choice. This means that early childhood educators in New York City, Chicago, Albuquerque, and Anchorage will celebrate many different holidays based on the children in their care. It means we can't give student teachers one answer to the question, "What is an appropriate approach to holidays?" We could also try to be less quick to judge each other as we try to determine our position on some of these tricky issues—and why.

Questions for Discussion

1. Do you celebrate holidays at your program? Which holidays? How do you decide which to acknowledge? Do the staff members agree that your program's approach to holidays is supportive of family wishes? How do you know?

2. Does the subject of what is politically or culturally appropriate for celebrations come up at staff meetings? Do people agree on what is appropriate? Do you wish for more or less discussion about these issues? Why?

3. How can we do a better job of respecting diversity without pinning ourselves into a corner with hard-and-fast notions that make teachers uncomfortable, such as don't say "tepee" and don't allow children to sing "Jingle Bells"?

A Place for Everyone

We've all had a professor, somewhere along the way, who has said, "The child you find most difficult to work with is the child who needs you the most." We are great at collecting mantras:

- Children first.

- Children are our future.

- Every child, a wanted child.

- Protect our natural resources: our children.

- Every child has special needs.

These statements probably increase our enthusiasm at conferences and remind us why we do the work we do. All of them ring of truth. All of them are important enough. And all of them highlight the educator's usual burden of having to bridge a theoretical concept with everyday practice!

For instance, we can say that children are our future and mean it in a deeply philosophical way. At the end of a ten-hour rainy day, however, and after being kicked in the shin and spit on by a four-year-old, many teachers might think, "I wish this child were in the future—five years away from my daily work life!"

We've all known, and greatly admired, the few wonderful teachers who truly have a calling to work with children who are difficult. Most of us just want to get through the day, keep the children safe, have some fun times, make a few exciting educational discoveries, and make enough money to pay a few bills! I'm sure I'm not the only one who has pretended not to see unacceptable behavior at the end of the day because I know that redirecting a particular child will set off a sequence of events I haven't the energy to deal with. I believe most of us have moments like this, even though we rarely have the confidence or the arena to share our feelings with one another. If I felt that way every day, of course, I would look into another kind of work.

We want to provide a caring community for all children, a place where children are safe and can learn and grow surrounded by people who know their quirks and still honor them. This noble idea is, in many ways, a great myth. Most teachers of young children don't like to say out loud that we don't like all children equally. Sometimes we feel scared and awkward because we don't know what to do with a child whose behavior is so disruptive we wish she were in another class. Let's face it, not all young children are sweet, adorable, cuddly, funny, and endearing. Still, a student in an entry-level early childhood education class is very likely to say things like, "I've just always wanted to work with young children because they are so cute, genuine, and loving." It's as likely for students to make this statement as it is for them to be indifferent to the wages they'll earn in the profession (see essay 4).

Some children learn before age three that no one can be trusted, that it is smarter to strike before you are struck, and that being nice makes you too vulnerable. Some children have tougher temperaments than others. Children who are treated well by adults often find it easy to treat others well. Children who have been hurt often find it easy to hurt others. I'd like to make it clear that when I say "children who have been hurt," I don't necessarily mean physically hurt, and I don't necessarily mean that the child has been mistreated by parents or caregivers. A difficult philosophical question of the ages is, why do some of us seem to have an easier ride than others? Children who are difficult to support in preschool might have been hurt by life because they live in poverty or because they live with a painful chronic illness. Or maybe while crossing the street hand in hand with her mother, the two-year-old's mother was hit by a car and killed. Regardless of the reason, when children are hurting, they feel like hurting back, which is not unlike many adults. But when children are continually grumpy, defiant, or hard to please, teachers and parents might feel discouraged. They might feel like failures. It can make the adults wish they were somewhere else.

Pediatrician T. Berry Brazelton gave parents a huge gift by saying out loud that it is easier to enjoy being the parent of an easygoing child than it is to enjoy being the parent of a challenging child. Nothing is harder for parents of feisty infants than seeing parents of easygoing infants in the supermarket, church, or library—or across the table at their mother-in-law's house—looking at them in a manner that says, "Why don't you do something to comfort her?" or "Make her be quiet." In fairness to parents blessed with easy-temperament children, our culture, conventional wisdom, and media give everyone the idea that sweet, smart, adorable children are the product of good parenting and teaching skills, whereas feistiness is the result of the opposite.

Once during a discussion in an early childhood course, the book *The Difficult Child* by Stanley Turecki (2000) came up. One of my students admitted that she had wanted to buy the book. She even had it in her hands at the bookstore (at this point in her story, she got very choked up), but she couldn't make herself take it to the checkout counter. She said buying the book seemed like an admission that she was not a good parent and that she thought poorly of her own child. It is poignant and heartbreaking for parents and children when daily routines are a source of great pain, angst, or turmoil.

The same is true for teachers who work with these children. Most educators believe they were not adequately prepared in teacher-training courses for dealing with children's behaviors. I have seen many young teachers with great promise leave the field for this reason. It just got too hard. They came in thinking they could make a difference for every child, and when they discovered that it was not always possible, they were heartbroken and found other work.

Much to my dismay, many teachers have never heard of the temperament studies by husband-and-wife team Alexander Thomas and Stella Chess (Thomas, Chess, and Birch 1968). Temperament has a huge impact on behavior and self-esteem, but it often receives minimal attention in child development texts. Stanley Turecki built his work on temperament from the foundation laid by Thomas and Chess. Turecki's books, such as *The Difficult Child,* keep alive Thomas and Chess's important work. Brazelton and others have also helped us see the many reasons why life or learning can be harder or easier for some of us than it is for others. I hear many providers say that young children's problematic behavior is intentional and mean, a deliberate effort to make providers crazy. This attitude is unfortunate for both teachers and the young children in their care. It takes a long time to learn the rules, expectations, and patterns of behavior of the culture in which one lives. As early childhood educators, we need to start talking with each other and with parents about what those expectations are.

Diana West (2007) wrote *The Death of the Grown-Up: How America's Arrested Development Is Bringing Down Western Civilization,* and I highly recommend this book to anyone working with families. In it, West discusses the turmoil in this country during the 1960s. She quotes researchers who think, along with her, that the cultural revolution of the 1960s did not result in a change to cultural boundaries. Instead, it resulted in the *loss* of cultural boundaries. For example, in essay 24, I describe reports from teachers who frequently hear families say, "I don't know what to do with my child." They hear parents respond to program concerns with statements like, "Well, he's just a small boy," instead of "How can we ALL make this better?" When children don't see that they aren't equals to their parents, we have not provided appropriate boundaries.

In *Stopping at Every Lemonade Stand: How to Create a Culture That Cares for Kids* (2001), James Vollbracht provides many simple ways we can adjust our attitudes about children and our society. When we talk about caring communities, we need to think classrooms, family child care neighborhoods, and the broader culture. If we care for children but disrespect their families—we fail. If we care for children but don't proactively teach them the norms and expectations of our culture—we fail. If we don't have a strong sense of what we expect in our culture, then we need to stop and figure it out. We are the grown-ups. We set the tone. We are responsible. If we don't accept that responsibility and act on it, we fail ourselves and our children.

We know how to care. We need to take time to do it—all of us! There are many who agree with me, including Jean Twenge (2006) author of *Generation Me: Why Today's Young Americans Are More Confident, Assertive, Entitled—and More Miserable Than Ever Before*. Twenge's book is a well-documented study of this generation's highly educated young adults. Twenge suggests that many of our country's problems are a result of the lack of positive environments that support families.

I view our field with optimism. Early childhood education is once again taking a positive step by stressing the importance of caring communities in our programs. Promoting caring communities, however, is easier said than done. Anne Stonehouse (1995) points out that when we truly partner with parents, we make our jobs harder. When we reach out to the difficult child in our group and don't give up on making that child part of our community, we contribute to a positive future for our country. When our professional skills include being respectful to *all* the children, not just the ones who are fun or easy to manage, we become our best selves and set a true example for the children in our care of what a caring community is all about. Most importantly, when we do this, we create a place for everyone.

Questions for Discussion

1. Have you ever worked in a program in which teachers played favorites? Describe what you saw that gave you this impression. What did you do about it?

2. What conditions might encourage teachers to treat children preferentially? Work as a team to develop a list of these conditions and a list of strategies that can help you work with your coteachers to eliminate this tendency.

3. Do you think Diana West is correct in suggesting that people in the United States have lost their cultural boundaries and expectations? If so, how come? If not, justify your more positive position.

Community Support: Do We Have It?

In 1979, my graduate school supervisor told me to find the book *Two Worlds of Childhood: U.S. and U.S.S.R.* by Urie Bronfenbrenner (1970). I had never heard of Bronfenbrenner. I had also never heard the word *ethnocentric*, let alone pondered whether I brought ethnocentric practices to my work with young children. As I read the book, I realized that over and over again in the tiniest of ways I had been learning what ethnocentric meant. Now, more than thirty years later, we frequently talk about ethnocentrism in classes and workshops addressing how best to meet the needs of the diverse families we serve. In the same way I marvel at how male-centric the field of psychology was for decades, I marvel at how our understanding of child growth and development was once almost solely informed by Western (European and United States) models. It is exciting to acknowledge how this is becoming less and less true with the passing of time.

It also amazes me how often new teachers tell me that they think they remember Bronfenbrenner (because it's such a unique name!), but they can't remember why they should know him or what contributions he's made to our field. It is not that Bronfenbrenner's ideas were totally original (Plato's *Republic* offers similar notions for living well), but to me he is the single contemporary theorist to put the cards on the table in a way that could redirect the course of humanity in a healthy and positive way.

Bronfenbrenner's theory of ecological systems puts an end to the nature versus nurture (heredity versus environment, genes versus experiences) debate. He clearly outlines the multiple factors that shape all humans in all cultures throughout time. If that statement captivates your interest, you will find adequate description of Bronfenbrenner's work in most human development or lifetime development texts. For the purpose of this essay, it's enough to say that Bronfenbrenner shows us that along with families, friends, schools, and communities, our children become who they become because of governments, cultures, values, media, moments in history, and myriad other factors we previously left out of the equation. We are all the solution to our problems!

I'm sure you've heard a colleague or family member say something like, "It's such a shame—the trouble she's in—and her parents are the salt of the earth. That's the last family you'd think would have to bail their daughter out of jail!" In the United States, we tend to blame individual parents or families for children's struggles without looking at the way our culture supports or contributes to the very problems we abhor. Juliet Schor (2005), economist and professor at Boston College, has carefully researched the ways marketing culture in this country has nurtured young people who believe they are what they own. In her book *We've Got Issues: Children and Parents in the Age of Medication*, Judith Warner (2010) documents the ways the medical profession and public education have turned their backs on families whose children struggle with mental health issues. Dr. Jean Twenge (2006, 7), herself a member of "generation me," writes, "Young people have been consistently taught to put their own needs first and to focus on feeling good about themselves. This is not an attitude conducive to following social rules or favoring the group's needs over the individual's."

One of the things so interesting about our culture is the way we think about children. Sadly, we think children are exclusively the responsibility of their parents—having nothing to do with the rest of us. Some people ask, "Why should I pay higher taxes for schools? I have no children!" The response might be, "Because one of today's children will perform your bypass surgery someday!" Today's children are tomorrow's leaders, parents, citizens, doctors, builders, and inventors, so we should *all* be interested in their well-being, good health, and education, even if only from selfish interest.

So many cultural groups—both in developed and underdeveloped countries—understand that "it takes a village to raise a child," but in the United States, we would rather reseed our lawn or send our doggie to daycare than invest in children's education. Someday, these children will make the policies that govern the treatment of the poor, sick, and elderly. If there is truth to the expression "What goes around comes around," some of us should be worried.

I have never been a fan of nostalgia. Though optimism and high expectations are important, so is realism. When we look at old reruns of *Father Knows Best* or *Leave It to Beaver* and say, "Those were the days!" we need to consider the reality of childhood in our country's history. In his book *Huck's Raft: A History of American Childhood*, Steven Mintz shares his meticulous research of US childhood through the decades. He writes, "To understand postwar childhood, it is essential to recognize that the period's family patterns—a high birthrate, a stable divorce rate, and a low number of mothers in the workforce—were a historical aberration, out of line with long-term historical trends" (Mintz 2004, 276).

Sociologists have been telling us this for decades. It is fascinating how we ignore this fact, imagining normal family life to be what is documented as a historical aberration. I remember how horrified family audiences were when *Roseanne* first aired. Those raised on Jim Anderson and Ward Cleaver bristled at the working-class Conner family who worked all day and then downed pizza for dinner in an informal fashion (instead of sitting at a "proper" table with a tablecloth, flowers, and a fresh-baked chicken). For me, the portrayal of a working mother of four kids was refreshing, as was seeing laundry and backpacks piled on the stairs and kids who didn't always respond to parental directives with "Yes, ma'am!"

On the first day of my sociology of the family courses, which I taught for many years, I always asked students to write whatever they wanted to tell me about their own families or about family life. I asked them to fill the front and back of one page. Without exception, at least half of the class would begin their comments with some variation of, "My family was no Brady Bunch, and we weren't like the Cosby's!" Decade after decade, books, films, and conventional wisdom perpetuate the image of an ideal family. I'm not sure I totally agree with Leo Tolstoy who tells us in *Anna Karenina* that "happy families are all alike; every unhappy family is unhappy in its own way."

I do know, after four decades of working with children and families by day and discussing families with college students by night, that it would be much more helpful if we openly acknowledge that most families are happy sometimes and very much in pain at other times. I would not begin to say there is equity in the family experience, but most of us will benefit when we eliminate stereotypes that encourage children to view their own families in a deficit model.

To return to Tolstoy, I do think that certain things make all happy families happy: affordable, high-quality child care, affordable and appropriate housing, enough food to eat, employment for parents, transportation, and good health care. These things do not come with a guarantee of happiness, but without them, focusing on other goals, such as worthwhile community or recreational projects, is impossible.

Who is responsible for the care of our children? How do we support family life and education for everyone in our communities and in our country? We can't make improvements until we make families a priority in our communities and schools. In *(Mis)Understanding Families: Learning from Real Families in Our Schools,* Marsh and Turner-Vorbeck (2010, 6–7) assert, "From the lack of request for parent voice, we see a belief that schooling is about children, outside of the context of their family and community." The authors go on to assert, as Bronfenbrenner has, that we cannot separate children from the context of their lives. Doing so, however, makes teacher's jobs much harder.

For example, I have served children whose families are passionate hunters, many of them for many generations. I always get that queasy "Oh no, someone shot Bambi" feeling when I pass a truck with a deer on top, as I often do in the fall. But working in rural New Hampshire communities means being respectful of this way of life that challenges my personal feelings. Part of my professional responsibility is to keep these personal feelings to myself.

When we look back at those sitcom families and feel tempted to use words like *broken home* in the staff room, we need to remember that family life is what it is. For many children, that means facing the reality of divorce as a fact of family life, not an aberration. Supporting children in the context of their families is our job. It doesn't matter what that family looks like, what they value, where they live, what language they speak, what their politics, faith, or tastes are. It is our job to welcome and respect *all* children and *all* of their families.

In her fine book *Generation Ex: Tales from the Second Wives Club*, Karen Karbo (2001) attempts to bridge the divorce gap for families. She provides lots of strategies for working with families in this new millennium. She states, "Long before divorce was so common, people were stuck in families they were born into, and the families they married into. . . . It was a given that every family had its share of detestable members. . . . You were forced to find a way to deal with them, whether it meant avoiding them, ignoring them, or humoring them. The fact that they were family didn't mean that you had to like them; it simply meant that you could hate them all you wanted to, but they weren't going anywhere" (Karbo 2001, 226–27). Karbo offers good advice to all of us who work with young families: "Never forget: Marriage, with children, really is forever. . . . There is, however, a bona fide reason for being civil and considerate to an ex you might normally despise: a child who loves him" (Karbo 2001, 226–27). She concludes by telling us that being civil to one another for the sake of children is a lot more valid that being nice to someone just because they happen to be your mother's uncle by marriage!

As we look for ways to be part of the village it takes to raise a child, we can all remind ourselves that a kind, considerate, empathic population of grown-ups will have a better chance of raising future citizens with those qualities than a group that can't bend. We don't have to break, mind you, but allowing ourselves to bend will be a huge first step to creating a better community and a better country.

Questions for Discussion

1. Should child care centers offer support to families beyond the eleven-hour child care day? Why or why not?

2. How do you interpret the well-known statement "It takes a village to raise a child"? Do you think every employee at your program could reach a consensus about what the expression should mean to all of you and the families you serve?

3. How do we stay true to our program's principles—such as "Dirty clothes means children learned a lot today!"—while honoring families who feel quite differently?

REFERENCES

Bank Street College of Education. 1981. *The Pleasure of Their Company: How to Have More Fun with Your Children*. Radnor, PA: Chilton.

Belsky, Jay, Deborah Lowe Vandell, Margaret Burchinal, Allison Clarke-Stewart, Kathleen McCartney, Margaret Tresch Owen, and the NICHD Early Child Care Research Network. 2007. "Are There Long-Term Effects of Early Child Care?" *Child Development* 78 (2): 681–701.

Bronfenbrenner, Urie. 1970. *Two Worlds of Childhood: U.S. and U.S.S.R.* New York: Russell Sage Foundation.

Bruno, Holly Elissa. 2007. "Gossip-Free Zone: Problem Solving to Prevent Power Struggles." *Young Children* 62 (5): 26–33.

Bruno, Holly Elissa, and Margaret Leitch Copeland. 1999. "If the Director Isn't Direct, Can the Team Have Direction?" *Leadership Quest* 3 (1): 6–8.

Carlsson-Paige, Nancy, and Diane E. Levin. 1990. *Who's Calling the Shots? How to Respond Effectively to Children's Fascination with War Play and War Toys*. Philadelphia, PA: New Society Publishers.

Carter, Margie. 2010. "Looking for Core Values." *Exchange*, no. 195: 18–21.

Carter, Margie, Sarah Felstiner, and Ann Pelo. 1999. *Thinking Big: Extending Emergent Curriculum Projects*. Mechanicsburg, PA: Harvest Resources.

Center on the Developing Child at Harvard University. 2010. *The Foundations of Lifelong Health Are Built in Early Childhood*. www.developingchild.harvard.edu.

Coontz, Stephanie. 1992. *The Way We Never Were: American Families and the Nostalgia Trap*. New York: Basic Books.

———. 1997. *The Way We Really Are: Coming to Terms with America's Changing Families*. New York: Basic Books.

Cowell, Jackie. 2011. "Finding Child Care in the Granite State." Interview by Laura Knoy. New Hampshire Public Radio, March 2. www.nhpr.org/finding-child-care-granite-state.

Elkind, David. 1981. *The Hurried Child: Growing Up Too Fast Too Soon*. Reading, MA: Addison-Wesley.

Feinburg, Sylvia G., and Mary Mindness. 1994. *Eliciting Children's Full Potential: Designing and Evaluating Developmentally Based Programs for Young Children*. Pacific Grove, CA: Brooks/Cole.

Galinsky, Ellen. 1999. *Ask the Children: What America's Children Really Think about Working Parents*. New York: HarperCollins.

Greenman, Jim. 1998. *Places for Childhood: Making Quality Happen in the Real World*. Redmond, WA: Exchange Press.

———. 2005. "Places for Childhood in the 21st Century: A Conceptual Framework." *Beyond the Journal, Young Children* 60 (3): 1–8. www .naeyc.org/files/yc/file/200505/01Greenman.pdf.

Ilg, Frances L., and Louise Bates Ames. 1972. *School Readiness: Behavior Tests Used at the Gesell Institute*. 2nd ed. New York: Harper and Row.

James, Susan Donaldson. 2008. "Preschoolers Behaving Badly: Expulsions Rise." ABC News, January 24. http://abcnews.go.com/US/story?id=4176434.

Jordan, June B., and Rebecca F. Dailey, eds. 1973. *Not All Little Wagons Are Red: The Exceptional Child's Early Years*. Arlington, VA: Council for Exceptional Children.

Karbo, Karen. 2001. *Generation Ex: Tales from the Second Wives Club*. New York: Bloomsbury.

Katz, Lilian. 1977. *Talks with Teachers: Reflections on Early Childhood Education*. Washington, DC: National Association for the Education of Young Children.

———. 1993. "Self-Esteem and Narcissism: Implications for Practice." ERIC Publications. ED358973. www.eric.ed.gov/ERICWebPortal/contentdelivery/servlet/ERICServlet?accno=ED358973.

———. 2010. "Knowledge, Understanding, and the Disposition to Seek Both." *Exchange*, no. 196: 46–47.

Kozol, Jonathan. 2007. *Letters to a Young Teacher*. New York: Three Rivers.

Marsh, Monica Miller, and Tammy Turner-Vorbeck. 2010. *(Mis)Understanding Families: Learning from Real Families in Our Schools*. New York: Teachers College Press.

McAlister, Anna R., and T. Bettina Cornwell. 2010. "Children's Brand Symbolism Understanding: Links to Theory of Mind and Executive Functioning." *Psychology and Marketing* 27 (3): 203–28.

Mintz, Steven. 2004. *Huck's Raft: A History of American Childhood*. Cambridge, MA: Belknap Press of Harvard University.

Moyers, Bill. 1988. Interview with Dr. T. Berry Brazelton. *A World of Ideas with Bill Moyers*.

National Education Association. 2011. "Myths and Facts about Educator Pay." Accessed June 30. www.nea.org/home/12661.htm.

Schor, Juliet. 2005. *Born to Buy: The Commercialized Child and the New Consumer Culture*. New York: Scribner.

Schweinhart, Lawrence J., Jeanne Montie, Zongping Xiang, William S. Barnett, Clive R. Belfield, and Milagros Nores. 2005. *Lifetime Effects: The HighScope Perry Preschool Study through Age 40.* Ypsilanti, MI: HighScope Press.

Stonehouse, Anne. 1995. *How Does It Feel? Child Care from a Parent's Perspective.* Redmond, WA: Exchange Press.

Tannen, Deborah. 1994. *Talking from 9 to 5: How Women's and Men's Conversational Styles Affect Who Gets Heard, Who Gets Credit, and What Gets Done at Work.* New York: Wm. Morrow.

Tate, Claudia, ed. 1983. *Black Women Writers at Work.* New York: Continuum.

Tavris, Carol. 1989. *Anger: The Misunderstood Emotion.* Rev. ed. New York: Simon and Schuster.

Thomas, Alexander, Stella Chess, and Herbert G. Birch. 1968. *Temperament and Behavior Disorders in Children.* New York: New York University Press.

Toffler, Alvin. 1970. *Future Shock.* New York: Random House.

Travers, Jeffrey et al. 1980. *Research Results of the National Day Care Study: Final Report of the National Day Care Study.* Vol. 2. Cambridge, MA: ABT Associates.

Turecki, Stanley. 2000. *The Difficult Child.* New York: Bantam Books.

Twenge, Jean M. 2006. *Generation Me: Why Today's Young Americans Are More Confident, Assertive, Entitled—and More Miserable Than Ever Before.* New York: Free Press.

Vollbracht, James. 2001. *Stopping at Every Lemonade Stand: How to Create a Culture That Cares for Kids.* New York: Penguin.

Warner, Judith. 2006. *Perfect Madness: Motherhood in the Age of Anxiety.* New York: Riverhead Books.

———. 2010. *We've Got Issues: Children and Parents in the Age of Medication.* New York: Riverhead Books.

West, Diana. 2007. *The Death of the Grown-Up: How America's Arrested Development Is Bringing Down Western Civilization.* New York: St. Martin's Griffin.

Wong, Harry K., and Rosemary T. Wong. 2009. *The First Days of School: How to Be an Effective Teacher.* 4th ed. Mountain View, CA: Harry K. Wong Publications.

Young-Eisendrath, Polly. 2008. *The Self-Esteem Trap: Raising Confident and Compassionate Kids in an Age of Self-Importance.* New York: Little, Brown.

C arol Garhart Mooney has a bachelor's degree in elementary education and a master's degree in early childhood education. She has completed coursework for a doctorate in sociology of the family. Carol began her teaching career in the inner city of Richmond, Virginia. As a college student, she volunteered in programs that helped involve children and families in their own communities. She also volunteered at the first trial run of Head Start programs in Washington, DC, which took place in 1965.

Her interest in early childhood education sprang from her own experiences as a mother of young children. She found the job of parenting and educating children to be more demanding than almost any other work; she is still surprised at the public perception that it's easy. While raising her young family, Carol completed her master's degree and ran two private preschools in New Hampshire, one in Londonderry and the other in Exeter. The Exeter school was also a full-day child care and family support center, and it was one of the first ten nationally accredited programs in New Hampshire. During those years, she was twice named the early childhood educator of the year and was honored with the New Hampshire Presswoman's Award for columns on family life. These columns were later published in a collection called *Reflections on Parenting*, published by the New England Association for the Education of Young Children.

Carol has been an instructor of early childhood education for thirty years at Granite State College. She is a recipient of their Distinguished Faculty Award. She worked for New Hampshire Head Start programs for nearly fifteen years, first as an itinerant instructor for their CDA (Child Development Associate) program and later as a manager and transition specialist for Belknap-Merrimack Head Start. She has supervised both student and practicing educators for more than twenty-five years. Carol also served as one of the first child care administrators for the New Hampshire Department of Health and Human Services. She is a board member of the New Hampshire Child

Care Advisory Committee, a member of Early Learning NH, and a past president of the New Hampshire Association for the Education of Young Children.

Carol's books *Theories of Childhood* and *Theories of Attachment* are very popular with students of early childhood education. Her volume on language, *Use Your Words*, is a favorite with child care providers. In *Swinging Pendulums*, she provides thoughtful essays on many provocative topics in the early childhood field as well as reflections on her daily work with children and their families. Her experience as a professor, administrator, classroom teacher, parent, and grandparent lend credibility to this diverse collection of essays.

Carol is the mother of four grown children, ranging in age from twenty-five to forty-one. She is the grandmother of two growing children. In other words, she has spent many years on both sides of the desk in parent-teacher conferences. In her spare time, she enjoys kayaking with her husband, Marc, and entertaining her large group of grown children and their children!